21 Ps™

THE WORLD'S

SUREST, COOLEST, FASTEST

BEST-RESULTS-SYSTEM

FOR MONEY & SUCCESS

IN MULTI-LEVEL/NETWORK MARKETING:

WHAT EVERY CONSUMER, PROSPECT

& MLM REPRESENTATIVE NEEDS!

By

Nelson Abaya
M.S., LEED AP

21PsMLM.com

21 Ps™

The World's Surest, Coolest, Fastest Best-Results-System In Multi-Level/Network Marketing:
What Every Consumer, Prospect & MLM Representative Needs!

Suggested Search Subject Headings:
1. Money and Success Systems
2. Network Marketing Systems
3. Multi-Level Marketing Programs
4. Direct Selling Systems and Training
5. Business Training Manuals
6. Network Marketing Companies
7. Prospecting and Business Building

I. Title: 21 Ps: The World's Surest, Coolest, Fastest Best-Results-System In Multi-Level/Network Marketing: What Every Consumer, Prospect & MLM Representative Needs!

Dedication,

To all the honest and hard-working MLM Representatives, Associates, Distributors and their Sponsors in Network Marketing's "Top 21" Nations (United States, Japan, Brazil, China, South Korea, Mexico, Germany, Italy, Russia, France, United Kingdom, Taiwan, Thailand, Canada, Columbia, Australia, Argentina, Malaysia, Venezuela, India and Singapore), may you fulfill your hopes and dreams through your daily contributions to family, community and country. You are what will make MLM the greatest Profession on the Planet!

21 Ps™

WORLD'S SUREST...FASTEST...SYSTEM FOR MONEY & SUCCESS...MLM CUSTOM GUIDEBOOK

TABLE OF CONTENTS

<u>21 Ps</u>™
WORLD'S SUREST...FASTEST...SYSTEM FOR MONEY & SUCCESS...MLM CUSTOM GUIDEBOOK

21 Ps™

WORLD'S SUREST...FASTEST...SYSTEM FOR MONEY & SUCCESS...MLM CUSTOM GUIDEBOOK

INTRODUCTION

The Multi-Level/Network Marketing (mostly referred to as MLM throughout this book) Industry is a phenomenon! MLM is now a $125 billion revenue business practiced in 150 countries through more than 75 million men and women as Representatives, Associates and Distributors every day!

In many economies, MLM is the one opportunity open to all, especially women and everyone even in the "richer" nations whose many citizens have endured recent monetary and social hardships. In boom times and downturns, Network Marketing has proven itself as a viable business model that has withstood the test of time and circumstance to become one of the best ways to secure a financial future for individuals and families.

The title of this book says it all! You who are involved in Network Marketing whether a newly minted MLM representative, a seasoned distributor/upline or someone who is being recruited to an MLM business or being sold its products or services, want something that you can use to succeed, save some dollars or make some or a lot of money! You yearn for the best results from a System that is sure, "cool" and fast!

This book is a Training Manual, a Sales-Prospecting Workbook, a Success Guide, a Consumer Handbook, a Recruiting Tool and a Personal/Life/Business Planner all in one! The Chapters are short but detailed with easy-to-do Exercises and Fill-in Forms that cover the entire process of analyzing, working, growing and succeeding in an MLM business. The ideas and methods in this book are presented and taught in an innovative unique mnemonic way to learn, remember and master Money & Success: the System of "21 Ps".

The "21 Ps" cover a complete system of business and "life" that includes how concepts are taught (3 Ps: Principles, Practices and Programs) in order to learn and apply the main ideas, methods and skills (15 Ps especially as they relate to MLM: Purpose, Productivity, Perseverance, Power, Patterning, Proposition, Product, People, Pricing, Pay, Prospecting, Presentations, Process, Promotions and Pinnacle of Success) and finally the superstructure of essential Ps (final 3 Ps of People or "Prosumers"-Consumers, Profits and Planet) that underlies everything.

The "21 Ps" have been developed from the established and time-tested methods and techniques of the most successful MLM Practitioners, Leaders and Trainers in the world, in addition to the principles and instructions of some of the greatest teachers in motivation, values and general success in life and business.

This book originated from a personal desire to learn about an industry and a way of life that I kept encountering. Throughout the years from childhood to young adulthood, I have seen the workings of MLM through family members and friends who were involved in the business. More and more I have been approached to consider many MLM products or services and opportunities. After doing preliminary research I wrote a Yahoo article (reproduced on Pages 155-156) that was meant to be a consumer article that allowed anyone to handle an MLM approach and to be able to find out the legitimacy of an MLM Company. After favorable reviews and ideas from Consumers and "MLM People" I undertook the writing of this Book.

It turns out that after extensive research there are indeed proven systems of money and success in MLM. Presented in various forms, formulas, guides and programs, many "universal truths" appeared. These universal Principles, Practices and Programs absolutely work! The only question is whether these systems are ever really learned and applied! To the ultimate objective of presenting a comprehensive system based on proven methods of money and success is *this* Book of "21 Ps". For fundamental and lasting achievement, may you learn and apply this system of "21 Ps" according to your purposes and motivations!

21 Ps™
WORLD'S SUREST...FASTEST...SYSTEM FOR MONEY & SUCCESS...MLM CUSTOM GUIDEBOOK

SECTION 1

THE MULTI-LEVEL/NETWORK MARKETING REPRESENTATIVE'S 5 "Ps"

THIS SECTION LAYS THE FOUNDATION FOR NEW OR ACHIEVEMENT-ORIENTED MLM REPRESENTATIVES (ALSO CALLED ASSOCIATES, DISTRIBUTORS, ETC.) AS WELL AS FOR SUCCESS-SEEKERS IN ANY CAREER FIELD OR ENTREPRENEURIAL ENDEAVOR.

THE 5 CHAPTERS THAT FOLLOW FORM THE BASIS OF LIFE AND UNIVERSAL SKILLS FOR SURVIVAL AND ULTIMATE ACHIEVEMENTS IN NETWORK MARKETING, BUSINESS IN GENERAL AND MODERN LIFE IN THE 21ST CENTURY.

THE PERSONAL DEVELOPMENT AND EMPOWERMENT LEARNED IN THE 5 Ps IN THIS SECTION WILL MAKE THE MASTERY OF MULTI-LEVEL/NETWORK MARKETING POSSIBLE AND IN FACT INEVITABLE.

21 Ps™
WORLD'S SUREST...FASTEST...SYSTEM FOR MONEY & SUCCESS...MLM CUSTOM GUIDEBOOK

BLANK PAGE FOR

SECTION 1

NOTES

21 Ps™

WORLD'S SUREST...FASTEST...SYSTEM FOR MONEY & SUCCESS...MLM CUSTOM GUIDEBOOK

CHAPTER 1
PURPOSE: WHO YOU ARE, WHAT YOU WANT and WHERE YOU'RE GOING

This Chapter will be the most important Chapter in the book, yet probably the most fun while being the least technical and mechanical. Purpose is ultimately the foundation of any (MLM) business, as well as any life that pursues prosperity, success and meaning.

The Exercises in this whole SECTION and in this Chapter will lay the groundwork for your overall achievements in MLM and beyond. Doing the following Exercises will put you on "auto pilot" for all your activities in setting up your business, prospecting-partnering, building and growing your team around you, and making sure the success you achieve will be in the context of a balanced life of health and happiness for yourself, your significant others, your community and planet.

Purpose resides within you. You must discover it. You must find out who you are. You are a product of your upbringing, your surroundings, your genes (only partly since in Chapter 4 you will discover that you can actually *control* your genes and biology), and your present perceptions of yourself (whether accurate or not or whether empowering or not). While Purpose lies within, it doesn't mean you don't have a choice to change it or don't have the conscious ability to truly refine it and manifest it.

Purpose lies at the heart of great and lasting achievement. Purpose unleashes energy and power. Purpose is manifested through goals which must be deliberate steps and actions that propel you each day. Goals become part of the MLM System of Money and Success that is the "21 Ps".

Purpose also equals motivation. Scientific studies show people's achievements come from the level of motivation, not the type or kind of motivation: Different people have different motivations, both big and small. Poignantly a similar degree of success for two individuals can for example happen from the motivation to succeed for their families as from the motivation to "show up" their families. What matters is how passionate one is in expressing and manifesting the motivation.

What are your truly driving motivations that will allow you or make you do whatever it takes to reach your true Purpose? Do you want to achieve total financial independence or just trying to make your mortgage or car payment? Do you want to educate yourself or your children in the best schools and programs? Or are you more passionate about teaching and exemplifying a steady income from a sustainable family business? Do you want to travel the world or make your community better from your financial and social contributions?

Purpose is intrinsically larger than yourself as it unfolds and develops. When you know the reasons behind what you want, you will find the ways and means to get the desired results! The purpose-driven life will construct your legacy (whatever that becomes). Will you leave *your* world a better place than you found it?

Once you find your driving motivations, large and small and "package" them into a Life Purpose, you are persistent in the moment, whatever the moment brings, and you will drive relentlessly *to* and *for* your destiny, however great your developed abilities, talent and your circumstances permit!

Purpose will then be driven by passion. You will hunger and crave for what you truly want. The urge to drive toward the impassioned Purpose will be almost an end itself. Your Purpose will then genuinely define you at your very core. "You got to do what you got to do". You are and will be unstoppable!

<u>21 Ps</u>™

WORLD'S SUREST...FASTEST...SYSTEM FOR MONEY & SUCCESS...MLM CUSTOM GUIDEBOOK

CHAPTER 1
PURPOSE: WHO YOU ARE, WHAT YOU WANT and WHERE YOU'RE GOING

PROGRAM EXERCISE 1:
What would I love to do or be if I did not have to worry about bills or obligations?

_____

_____

_____

_____

_____

_____

_____

_____

_____

_____

_____

_____

_____

_____

-This is a wide open Exercise to explore your dreams, beliefs and wants from your past or present. Delve into what would be your ideal livelihood or career or life situation. You can fantasize and be totally fun or serious to bring out your inner desires. This can help you in later Exercises to start you thinking beyond your current circumstances and any limiting attitudes and beliefs. Anything is possible!-

21 Ps™

WORLD'S SUREST...FASTEST...SYSTEM FOR MONEY & SUCCESS...MLM CUSTOM GUIDEBOOK

PURPOSE: WHO YOU ARE, WHAT YOU WANT and WHERE YOU'RE GOING

PROGRAM EXERCISE 2A:
What would I do with $5 Million (beyond paying bills or taxes)? What would I buy? What would I build? How much would I give, if any and to whom, if anyone? Where would I live or where would I go?

_____

_____

_____

_____

_____

_____

_____

PROGRAM EXERCISE 2B:
On a less grand scale, but also revealing of core values, motivations and purpose, what would I do if I had $50,000 in cash that must be only spent or given (not saved or to be used to pay bills) today? What would I buy? Who would I give to, if anyone? What would I do?

_____

_____

_____

_____

_____

_____

_____

_____

21 Ps™

WORLD'S SUREST...FASTEST...SYSTEM FOR MONEY & SUCCESS...MLM CUSTOM GUIDEBOOK

CHAPTER 1
PURPOSE: WHO YOU ARE, WHAT YOU WANT and WHERE YOU'RE GOING

PROGRAM EXERCISE 3:
If I only had 6 months to live, what would I do before I die? (I would be able to function normally without any physical limitations or pain and be able to use the resources and abilities that I already have.)

_____

_____

_____

_____

_____

_____

_____

_____

_____

_____

_____

_____

_____

_____

_____

_____

_____

21 Ps™

WORLD'S SUREST...FASTEST...SYSTEM FOR MONEY & SUCCESS...MLM CUSTOM GUIDEBOOK

PRINCIPLE EXERCISE 4:
LIFE PURPOSE STATEMENT
Using words with thought and care and from everything that I learned about myself in the previous
Exercises, the following one or two concise paragraphs define MY PURPOSE in life:

(What you write below will be your mission or credo in your personal, business and spiritual lives. You can make this private or public but be careful in your formulation of your LIFE PURPOSE because its creation and existence will drive you forward to behaviors, beliefs and goals that will be manifested in some form of reality, whether in part or in its entirety! Be careful in what you conceive, you WILL get it! For practical matters, with regard to the MLM opportunity you are engaged in or considering, ask yourself if your LIFE PURPOSE fits the business, the people and the environment. Either DO NOT do the business and look for another opportunity and life situation or if you believe in the opportunity make your LIFE PURPOSE and the MLM business fit!)

_____

_____

_____

_____

_____

_____

_____

_____

_____

_____

_____

_____

-Take your time in doing your LIFE PURPOSE Statement; You may have to tweak it or adjust it over time and circumstance, but you should create something enduring you can refer to constantly and joyfully that comes from deep inside your beliefs and desires!-

21 Ps™

WORLD'S SUREST...FASTEST...SYSTEM FOR MONEY & SUCCESS...MLM CUSTOM GUIDEBOOK

CHAPTER 1
PURPOSE: WHO YOU ARE, WHAT YOU WANT and WHERE YOU'RE GOING

PROGRAM EXERCISE 5:
GOALS: WHERE YOU'RE GOING & <u>WHEN</u>:
Now that you have stated a LIFE PURPOSE, set SPECIFIC GOALS that have definite Time Frames and Deadlines. This Exercise will list your Goals in all areas you wish to accomplish from Personal to Professional to Spiritual. Include an explicit time for you to accomplish the Goal such as "in 6 months, I will lose 20 pounds" or "in 1 year, I will earn at least $5,000 *more* per month", or "in 2 years I will be debt-free", or "starting next week, I will devote at least half a day every week with a loved one for personal activities and quality time", etc. Describe in your Goal what specific tasks you have to do, what you have to change to accomplish the Goal, and how important the Goal is to your LIFE PURPOSE.

GOAL 1:

_____

_____

_____

_____

_____

_____

GOAL 2:

_____

_____

_____

_____

_____

_____

21 Ps™

WORLD'S SUREST...FASTEST...SYSTEM FOR MONEY & SUCCESS...MLM CUSTOM GUIDEBOOK

PURPOSE: WHO YOU ARE, WHAT YOU WANT and WHERE YOU'RE GOING

GOAL 3:

_____

_____

_____

_____

_____

GOAL 4:

_____

_____

_____

_____

_____

GOAL 5:

_____

_____

_____

_____

_____

You can "schedule" your Goals and Successes on your Hourly Calendar starting on page 160 and on the forms in SPECIAL TOOLS 1 on a monthly, 3-month, 6-month, yearly, 2-year, 3-year, 5-year, 10-year, 25-year and 50-year basis!

21 Ps™

WORLD'S SUREST...FASTEST...SYSTEM FOR MONEY & SUCCESS...MLM CUSTOM GUIDEBOOK

CHAPTER 1
PURPOSE: WHO YOU ARE, WHAT YOU WANT and WHERE YOU'RE GOING

REMINDERS / NOTES / EXTRA SPACE FOR EXERCISES:

_____

_____

_____

_____

_____

_____

_____

_____

_____

_____

_____

_____

_____

_____

_____

_____

21 Ps™

WORLD'S SUREST...FASTEST...SYSTEM FOR MONEY & SUCCESS...MLM CUSTOM GUIDEBOOK

CHAPTER 2
PRODUCTIVITY: ENERGY, EFFICIENCY and EFFECTIVENESS

Engaged and excited by your (just refined) Life Purpose, you are ready to conquer the world! What do you need to do? How will you go about creating success in your new Network Marketing Business? Or in other areas of your life?! The mechanics of the Money and Success System will be illustrated and learned in subsequent Ps in SECTIONS 1 and 2. In this Chapter, you have to keep building and strengthening your foundation: learning and practicing PRODUCTIVITY by managing Energy and gaining Efficiency and ultimately achieving Effectiveness. Embodied in PRODUCTIVITY are such Principles and Practices as Self-Discipline, Faith, Attitude and Work Ethic.

ENERGY

To be productive, one must have the consistent energy that derives from purpose and passion that in turn drives more motivation and energy. Physical, emotional and spiritual energy are required to be able to work the business that consists of the knowledge, techniques, tools and sequence of steps that you will be taught and trained.

You must have a minimum level of physical fitness that you must gain or improve in order to prepare yourself for the challenges and rigors of achievement. For example, if you do not have a physical exercise program, start at the most basic: walk for at least 15 to 30 minutes, *every* day if possible. Create a routine that must be habit. If you already have an exercise regimen, improve it if possible, including some simple "weight training" that can consist of hand barbells (starting light and a minimum of 30 total repetitions – a matter of 5 minutes that can increase by weight and duration as you progress.)

Energy levels are affected by what you eat, how much rest and exercise you get, your surroundings especially the people around you be they family, friends or associates, and most importantly by your emotions and perspectives on your life and circumstances. These factors are discussed later in this Chapter. But first you must make an inventory of your energy states and their sources.

PROGRAM EXERCISE 1:
What are your usual Energy Levels (from 1, very low to 10 very high) in different areas of your life:
-When working, at home or outside, at different times of day and different times of the week-

_____

_____

_____

_____

_____

21 Ps™

WORLD'S SUREST...FASTEST...SYSTEM FOR MONEY & SUCCESS...MLM CUSTOM GUIDEBOOK

CHAPTER 2
PRODUCTIVITY: ENERGY, EFFICIENCY and EFFECTIVENESS

PROGRAM EXERCISE 2:
List and briefly describe the positive and negative sources of personal Energy that you experience
-Examples are positive and inspirational friends and the opposite; also meditation and exercise, etc.-

_____

_____

_____

_____

_____

EFFICIENCY

The mechanics of being Efficient that leads to PRODUCTIVITY in the most basic ways are functions of time-management and your work ethic.   Starting on Page 160, The Weekly Calendar is a Scheduling/Planning tool that should include "To-Dos" (and also "Not-To-Dos"!) of explicit tasks as well as the Goals you established from your LIFE PURPOSE in Chapter 1. The week is used as the foundational unit of measurement (encompassing 7 full days) that can be conceived of as continuous, synergistic and adjustable to build to a month, quarter year, half-year, year and more.

PROGRAM EXERCISE 3:
Analyze your time efficiency and whether you get things done as you would like to in terms of its timeliness (on time as you would like?) and quality (are you satisfied with the results and how they relate to your overall Goals and LIFE PURPOSE?).

_____

_____

_____

_____

_____

_____

_____

21 Ps™

WORLD'S SUREST...FASTEST...SYSTEM FOR MONEY & SUCCESS...MLM CUSTOM GUIDEBOOK

CHAPTER 2
PRODUCTIVITY: ENERGY, EFFICIENCY and EFFECTIVENESS

EFFECTIVENESS

In one of the most influential and greatest works on achievement and success, *The 7 Habits of Highly Effective People*, by Steven Covey, (revised in 2004 with over 15 million copies sold!), 3 of the Habits relate to Effectiveness and ultimate PRODUCTIVITY (labeled, "Personal Victory"): "Be Proactive", "Begin with the End in Mind", and "Put First Things First". The rest of the Exercises in this Chapter explore these "habits" for Effectiveness.

PRINCIPLE EXERCISE 4:
Answer the following questions, briefly explaining any points.

Do you feel you take responsibility for your own actions? Cite any positive or negative examples.
Rate yourself on a scale of between 1 to 5 (1 being the "least" and 5 being the "most") in terms of your responsibility for your current actions.

_____

_____

_____

_____

_____

_____

Do you seek and accept Challenges? Cite any positive and negative examples. Rate yourself on a scale of between 1 to 5 (1 being the "least willing" and 5 being the "most ready") in terms of your willingness and readiness to take on any Challenges.

_____

_____

_____

_____

_____

_____

21 Ps™

WORLD'S SUREST...FASTEST...SYSTEM FOR MONEY & SUCCESS...MLM CUSTOM GUIDEBOOK

CHAPTER 2
PRODUCTIVITY: ENERGY, EFFICIENCY and EFFECTIVENESS

PROGRAM EXERCISE 5
List the priorities in your Life and in your MLM business. What comes first for you? You probably know what you need to do in your MLM business to succeed. List those things you know that you need to do. Are there conflicts among your priorities? Can you work them out? Are you efficient and ultimately effective enough to reach your Goals?

_____

_____

_____

_____

_____

_____

_____

_____

_____

_____

_____

_____

_____

_____

_____

_____

21 Ps™

WORLD'S SUREST...FASTEST...SYSTEM FOR MONEY & SUCCESS...MLM CUSTOM GUIDEBOOK

CHAPTER 2
PRODUCTIVITY: ENERGY, EFFICIENCY and EFFECTIVENESS

Very revealing are industry statistics on the number of hours worked by the average MLM Representative (over 16 million in U.S. and 75 million worldwide according to the World Federation of Direct Selling Associations, 2011): the "majority" work less than 5 hours per week! Even "part-time" of 25 hours per week applied consistently does lead to success. In fact there are really only about 25 "golden hours" in MLM because the most productive hours are usually only about 5 hours for 4 days during the regular week and another 5 hours on weekends.

PRACTICE EXERCISE 6
Accurately examine your actual work hours and put down the actual number of hours (if any) for each day of the week and the actual activity that you did. This Book's SECTION 3 will provide more details in such areas as Prospecting, Presentations, Follow-ups and Meetings/Trainings. Look at the Weekly Timelines in your Calendar to provide a perspective on your planning and scheduling. In this Exercise list your concrete activities and describe whether you are spending enough time working your business or achieving your Goals and if not, why not. Are your results not satisfactory or are you just not working enough hours? Why or why not?

_____

_____

_____

_____

_____

_____

_____

_____

_____

_____

_____

_____

_____

_____

_____

21 Ps™
WORLD'S SUREST...FASTEST...SYSTEM FOR MONEY & SUCCESS...MLM CUSTOM GUIDEBOOK

CHAPTER 2
PRODUCTIVITY: ENERGY, EFFICIENCY and EFFECTIVENESS

REMINDERS / NOTES / EXTRA SPACE FOR EXERCISES:

_____

_____

_____

_____

_____

_____

_____

_____

_____

_____

_____

_____

_____

_____

_____

_____

_____

_____

21 Ps™

WORLD'S SUREST...FASTEST...SYSTEM FOR MONEY & SUCCESS...MLM CUSTOM GUIDEBOOK

CHAPTER 3
PERSEVERANCE: PERSISTING, SELF-CORRECTING and NEVER GIVING UP

If Productivity allows you a certain degree of success and a measure of results from your Energy, Efficiency and Effectiveness, how do you sustain and build on any level of accomplishment? How do you move forward in the MLM business (and Life) which inevitably involves "Failure" (defined basically as not *yet* getting the results you want such as not being able to sponsor enough people, if any at all, or not finding enough customers for your MLM product or service and thus not making the income that you envisioned)?

Perseverance is the answer! Perseverance in the field of network marketing and other spheres of human endeavor means Persisting and going forward no matter what (Never Giving Up) and thus allowing for the opportunity for Self-Correcting to get the desired results that are encompassed in your Goals from your Life Purpose.

Life and business are all about "failure" (again simply defined as not getting desired results *as of yet*) and overcoming failure. "Failures" lead to experience and learning. Every skill and ability we possess stemmed from not yet knowing or from trial and error. Often however we know the reasons why we did not get the results desired. We did not persist. We were unprepared or deficient in some skill or we did not practice self-discipline. Nonetheless we know that the particular "failed" result can change to a positive income by persisting or self-correcting.

Self-discipline is in fact a key component to Perseverance. Self- discipline to do what it takes to learn, act and execute is very much related to the Life Purpose which you have developed. It is much easier to delay gratification if doing the non-expedient thing is driven by the long perspective of meeting your goals and supporting your Life Purpose. What may seem difficult and "not fun" can somehow be undertaken because the temporary sacrifice of indulgence today is traded in for the Purpose-driven pleasures of a brighter future!

Some transcendent areas of self-discipline are supportive of the Life Purpose and its goals. Areas such as exercise, eating, physical appearance, punctuality, procrastination, meeting deadlines, work ethic and self-improvement must be mastered or improved with self-discipline and training.

Practically speaking you must be as fit and healthy, and as professional as possible. One quick practical tip regarding procrastination for example is to tackle and finish 1 or 2 of the "toughest jobs" first to get momentum, feel good and feel confident and thus make the rest of your "chores" or "to-dos" easier. Perseverance in the face of obstacles or hardships separates the accomplished MLM Practitioner from those who have yet mastered the attitudes and skills of persistence, self-correction and never giving up.

This Chapter includes Program Exercises dealing with "Failures" and learning from them. Other Exercises will be ones on self-analysis with regard to your general strengths and weaknesses, as well as Exercises on specific self-evaluations of your skills in your MLM business. Strengths will be useful starting points for maximizing your results while weaknesses will be worked on by Principles, Practices and Programs in the areas of Self-Discipline and Self-Confidence developed from (self) study, training and support from your mentors and Team/Company Leaders which you will eventually duplicate and be able to teach others as well.

<u>21 Ps</u>™

WORLD'S SUREST...FASTEST...SYSTEM FOR MONEY & SUCCESS...MLM CUSTOM GUIDEBOOK

CHAPTER 3
PERSEVERANCE: PERSISTING, SELF-CORRECTING and NEVER GIVING UP

PROGRAM EXERCISE 1
List and describe 1 or 2 past "Failures" (not getting the results you desired). What happened and what did you learn? What positives developed from these "Failures"? What do you think were some of the causes of the "Failure"? Attempt to look into possible *personal* shortfalls and weaknesses and minimize any blame on circumstances or other people. Recall the Program Exercise in Chapter 2 regarding "Proactivity" and taking personal responsibility. You will be able to explore "Weaknesses" in Program Exercise 4 later in this Chapter.

_____

_____

_____

_____

_____

_____

_____

_____

_____

_____

_____

_____

_____

_____

_____

_____

_____

_____

21 Ps™

WORLD'S SUREST...FASTEST...SYSTEM FOR MONEY & SUCCESS...MLM CUSTOM GUIDEBOOK

PROGRAM EXERCISE 2
Explore in some detail one of your Goals from Chapter 1. Describe what your feelings would be (if) when you have actually accomplished the Goal. What would it mean for you, your family and business/work? What would be some of the "rewards" you would give yourself if you made the Goal? What would be some of the possible obstacles and hardships that you might face? Would you do what was necessary to reach your Goal?

_____

_____

_____

_____

_____

_____

_____

PROGRAM EXERCISE 3
With the described Goal in the above Exercise, act as if you were mentoring or coaching someone else who had the same above Goal. What would you advise as the necessary requirements to accomplish the Goal above? How would you help or support the Goal-Setter if you were a friend, mentor or business-partner?

_____

_____

_____

_____

_____

_____

_____

21 Ps™

WORLD'S SUREST...FASTEST...SYSTEM FOR MONEY & SUCCESS...MLM CUSTOM GUIDEBOOK

CHAPTER 3
PERSEVERANCE: PERSISTING, SELF-CORRECTING and NEVER GIVING UP

What is working for you in business (and life) and what is NOT working well? You have to know your weaknesses and how to eliminate or improve them. Examples are deficiencies in communication (how you come across or how you approach prospects or potential customers) or lack of follow-through or lack of product knowledge or poor time-management.

PROGRAM EXERCISE 4
Honestly consider, list and analyze 2 or 3 of your weaknesses below and describe possible solutions.

_____

_____

_____

_____

_____

_____

_____

_____

_____

_____

_____

_____

_____

_____

Honest self-analysis is sometimes difficult to undertake or achieve. A powerful but perhaps humbling way to look at weaknesses (and also strengths) is to ask a respected friend or mentor (or MLM Sponsor) to help you evaluate what is working and *not* working for you and to find solutions or improvements. The friend or mentor or MLM Sponsor will have a strong motivation to help you because of friendship or because of business self-interest.

21 Ps™

WORLD'S SUREST...FASTEST...SYSTEM FOR MONEY & SUCCESS...MLM CUSTOM GUIDEBOOK

PROGRAM EXERCISE 5

List at least 2 examples of an Accomplishment in your Life (Personal, School or Work/Business) where you overcame hardships, obstacles, and any initial "failure(s)". The examples can be about something you consider important (even if "small") and worth the struggles undertaken.

_____

_____

_____

_____

_____

_____

_____

_____

_____

_____

_____

_____

_____

_____

_____

_____

_____

_____

_____

21 Ps™

WORLD'S SUREST...FASTEST...SYSTEM FOR MONEY & SUCCESS...MLM CUSTOM GUIDEBOOK

CHAPTER 3
PERSEVERANCE: PERSISTING, SELF-CORRECTING and NEVER GIVING UP

REMINDERS / NOTES / EXTRA SPACE FOR EXERCISES:

_____

_____

_____

_____

_____

_____

_____

_____

_____

_____

_____

_____

_____

_____

_____

_____

_____

21 Ps™

WORLD'S SUREST...FASTEST...SYSTEM FOR MONEY & SUCCESS...MLM CUSTOM GUIDEBOOK

CHAPTER 4
POWER: PERSONAL and EXTERNAL, PUSHED TO TOP LEVELS

CONCEPT OF POWER

Purpose, Productivity and Perseverance are encompassed in the powerful concept of Power, in the Personal and External areas that are critical for Money and true Success in Multi-Level/Network Marketing (and Life!).

Power can be defined as "the ability to produce the results you desire most and create value for others in the process. Power is the ability to change your life, to shape your perceptions, to make things work for you and not against you. Real power is shared, not imposed. It's the ability to define human needs and to fulfill them—both your needs and the needs of the people you care about. It's the ability to direct your own personal kingdom—your own thought processes, your own behavior—so you produce the precise results your desire" (Anthony Robbins, *Unlimited Power: The New Science of Personal Achievement*, Free Press, Revised for Amazon Kindle, 2008)

This Chapter will explore your Beliefs and Communications (both internal and external) and the actions that ensue to create the results you desire and target. You will look into areas of self-management that you can then apply to the management of your MLM business and MLM team after refining or changing your perceptions and beliefs to empowering ones that lead to the true overall Success you desire.

Science has revealed many secrets and insights into the Power of Beliefs and the Biology and Physics/Chemistry of Consciousness both from the standpoint of the practical Psychology of the conscious mind and the biochemical aspects of the vast subconscious which may require reprogramming and various "scientific" strategies such as nutrition, exercise and meditation.

SCIENCE OF BELIEFS, STATES and EMPOWERMENT

It turns out that Beliefs control Biology! The approximately 50 Trillion single cells that make up a human being respond directly to the Brain whose states are governed by Beliefs and Self-Perceptions. While most of biology is automatic and results from the vast power of the subconscious nervous system, the conscious mind can reprogram the subconscious through various means. Once the subconscious is harnessed and congruent with empowering Beliefs, anything and everything is possible!

Science continues to march forward and findings about the capabilities of the human mind and human spirit continue to amaze and are just being discovered for applications in personal development and achievement. One of the most fertile areas of scientific inquiry is the field of Epigenetics which study the molecular mechanisms by which environment controls gene activity.

It has been proven scientifically that beliefs control our bodies, our minds and thus our lives! Empowering thoughts, ideas and beliefs have a profound effect on behavior and genes (the very basis and instructions for life) when they are in harmony with subconscious programming (found to be 20 million times more powerful than the conscious mind). Ultimately however, "the fully conscious mind trumps both nature and nurture" (Bruce Lipton, Ph.D., *The Biology of Belief: Unleashing the Power of Consciousness, Matter, & Miracles*, Mountain of Love/Elite Books, 2005).

21 Ps™

WORLD'S SUREST...FASTEST...SYSTEM FOR MONEY & SUCCESS...MLM CUSTOM GUIDEBOOK

CHAPTER 4
POWER: PERSONAL and EXTERNAL, PUSHED TO TOP LEVELS

BELIEFS

The abilities we unleash, the results we accomplish from the actions we engage in start with our own Internal Beliefs. These beliefs may be true or false, empowering or debilitating but we hold them as our own and have developed these convictions from different sources starting from our upbringing/parenting, to our friends, to our past experiences and to our own "learning".

PROGRAM EXERCISE 1A
You have to know and examine your beliefs, especially the negative or disempowering beliefs that will not serve you in getting the results you want. For example: "I am not smart enough"; or "I am not a born salesperson"; or "I am not a good speaker"; or "I am not educated enough"; or "I am not just not a go-getter"; or "I don't have enough time"; etc.
List your disempowering beliefs below, especially as they relate to your MLM business:

_____

_____

_____

_____

PROGRAM EXERCISE 1B
Now list some empowering or positive Beliefs that could help you in your quest for better or optimum results:
(For example: "I am resourceful and highly motivated"; "I can apply the proper sales and marketing techniques that fit my style and personality"; "I can learn the MLM business and my company's products and plans extremely well to give me confidence"; "I have the courage and power to start and sustain my MLM business until I succeed"; etc.)

_____

_____

_____

_____

Sometimes it is powerful enough to stop or eliminate negative and disempowering Beliefs. Often what replaces a false and damaging Belief will disprove it or allow one to get knowledge or perspective to change harmful Beliefs to vitalizing Beliefs.

21 Ps™

WORLD'S SUREST...FASTEST...SYSTEM FOR MONEY & SUCCESS...MLM CUSTOM GUIDEBOOK

CHAPTER 4
POWER: PERSONAL and EXTERNAL, PUSHED TO TOP LEVELS

COMMUNICATIONS: INTERNAL

To further examine your Beliefs (negative and positive) you have to be aware of your "internal communications", what your internal states are and what your internal representations are with regard to a particular Belief. Beliefs and their attendant perceptions and actions/reactions are often on autopilot. Remember the enormous power of the subconscious: 20 million times more potent than the conscious mind or will power! You would need powerful reprogramming (personal and with the help of a support group) and the mysterious power of Faith to overcome some of your destructive Beliefs that will dissipate in influence once you replace them with empowering Beliefs that when good results are produced will simultaneously disprove your deeply ingrained negative Beliefs.

PROGRAM EXERCISE 2

What are some of your internal states with various Beliefs you have? How do you feel about yourself? What is the internal image you have of your abilities and self-worth? How do you "communicate" with yourself?

_____

_____

_____

_____

COMMUNICATIONS: EXTERNAL

When you interact with the outside world, you are revealing yourself with your appearance, your language and ultimately you behavior. In the world of MLM, support "networks" are readily available to help you improve your skills and results, all to the benefit of the Team and you. The Book's SECTION 3 will go into detail in the empowerment of "Team" where you can gain great value, collaboration and profits!

PROGRAM EXERCISE 3

In the area of language for example, describe your external communications with your Sponsors, downline, customers and prospects. How can you improve your language of success and achievement? Even single words elicit powerful ideas and images. For example the word "selling" might be better stated and perceived as "sharing", or "prospecting" might be appropriately replaced by "potential partnering" just as "recruiting" might best be explained and termed as "sponsoring" or "mentoring" or "training".

_____

_____

_____

_____

21 Ps™

WORLD'S SUREST...FASTEST...SYSTEM FOR MONEY & SUCCESS...MLM CUSTOM GUIDEBOOK

CHAPTER 4
POWER: PERSONAL and EXTERNAL, PUSHED TO TOP LEVELS

SELF-MANAGEMENT: OVERCOMING OBSTACLES

Personal Power will emanate from the management of Inner States and Internal Representations that will be reactions or perspectives to what happens daily in your MLM business. To reach a top level of achievement, you will have to cope with the inevitable challenges that surface as you present your business opportunity, grow your team and administer your available resources.

PROGRAM EXERCISE 4
List the obstacles and hurdles that you are facing or think you will face in your MLM business. Describe specific Frustrations, Rejections and Self-Doubts and their possible Solutions.

_____

_____

_____

_____

_____

SELF-MANAGEMENT: REPROGRAMMING

Without resorting to any elaborate psychotherapy or "mental reconditioning", you can start to work on your Inner States and Internal Representations with positive lifestyle changes such as better physical fitness and nutrition, stress-reduction programs that might include meditation, prayer and massage. The immense power of the subconscious can be used in your favor to develop empowering states, attitudes and Beliefs that can lead to proactive actions, corrections and self-development towards results and Personal Power. Self-management will also have an external component as discussed in this Chapter's final Exercise (next Page) as well as the supportive environment of success that is the objective of the MLM Team's "5Ps" in SECTION 3.

PROGRAM EXERCISE 5
What are your current strategies of self-development, stress-reduction and personal/physical improvement? List the days and hours spent on various "reprogramming" and incorporate them into your Calendar in the back of this Book, and also starting on page 107, Special Tools 1: "Time-Lines of Goals and Successes".

_____

_____

_____

_____

21 Ps™

WORLD'S SUREST...FASTEST...SYSTEM FOR MONEY & SUCCESS...MLM CUSTOM GUIDEBOOK

SELF-MANAGEMENT: EXTERNALIZING OBSTACLES WITH TEAM SUPPORT

As a brief introduction to the concept of "Team" in your MLM business, your success in self-management will be aided or perhaps even hindered by your Sponsors and upline. Duplicating what is successful is the subject of the next Chapter and the support structure of the MLM Team will be covered in detail in SECTION 3. You can apply leadership skills in your MLM Team even as you start out. You can foster your personal excellence and the Team's (especially your downline's) overall performance by looking for support and maximizing training and leadership-development for everyone.

PROGRAM EXERCISE 6

Analyze your MLM Team's performance as you currently view it. Are there any structural problems from your standpoint? Seek or help to overcome any team inertia (lack of activity or group spirit or organizational purpose). Seek advice and counsel from your Sponsor/Upline. Depending on the MLM Company's growth stage, the elements of innovation, focus or teamwork may differ. So long as the Patterning and Modeling (Duplicating) of Success (to be covered in Chapter 5) is not violated, seek and expect enthusiasm, new ideas and creativity from the environment provided by your MLM Team.

_____

_____

_____

_____

_____

_____

_____

_____

_____

_____

_____

_____

_____

_____

21 Ps™

WORLD'S SUREST...FASTEST...SYSTEM FOR MONEY & SUCCESS...MLM CUSTOM GUIDEBOOK

CHAPTER 4
POWER: PERSONAL and EXTERNAL, PUSHED TO TOP LEVELS

REMINDERS / NOTES / EXTRA SPACE FOR EXERCISES:

_____

_____

_____

_____

_____

_____

_____

_____

_____

_____

_____

_____

_____

_____

_____

_____

_____

_____

21 Ps™

WORLD'S SUREST...FASTEST...SYSTEM FOR MONEY & SUCCESS...MLM CUSTOM GUIDEBOOK

CHAPTER 5
PATTERNING and MODELING: DUPLICATING SUCCESS, THE KEY TO MLM

NUMBER ONE KEY TO MLM SUCCESS

Every long-term prosperous MLM organization of every service or product line, without exception, owes its success to Duplication (Patterning and Modeling what is successful).

MLM promotes and rewards Duplication because its business model requires the exposure and marketing, sales and distribution (of information and products/services), and training of its participants (Representatives or Distributors or Associates) across wide and deep organizations that is diversified in backgrounds, experiences and motivations.

Duplication (Patterning and Modeling) in MLM can be defined as: <u>Leading and motivating an ever enlarging group of impassioned people to perform the same steps and actions consistently and continuously toward success!</u> Only with Duplication can an MLM Company's system be presented, implemented and executed in the most efficient and effective way.

There are no viable shortcuts to MLM success, nor any new-fangled way to create a large and vibrant MLM organization that rewards its Leaders with continuous large residual incomes other than Duplication. Not even sheer talent or charisma or an extreme work ethic can build long-lasting sustainable success in MLM.

In fact, phenomenal talent, amazing charisma and super human work ethic are impossible to duplicate continuously or consistently! An incredible organization may be built by a truly great Leader, but if the Leader cannot teach and have his or her unique skills and actions duplicated, the organization's success and attendant large incomes will all be short-lived!

Ideally, the successful MLM practitioner will become a Leader and teach others (especially his downline) to be Leaders like him or her. A Leader will develop other Leaders to replace him or her, thus allowing for the freedom to develop other Leaders and to enjoy the rewards of success which will be money and time for family, pleasure and personal development.

This Chapter will cover the elements of duplication which are the patterning and modeling of belief and value systems (of already successful MLM Leaders); the duplication of the exact sequence of steps in the MLM Company's system of exposure, presentation, marketing/distribution, as well as training and development; the proper use and sequence of tools, materials and resources made available by the MLM Company and the MLM Representative's Team; and finally the principles and philosophy of Duplication which are to be held "sacred" as a system.

Money and true success in MLM will result in building large and highly profitable organizations that sustain themselves with a system for any new Representatives or long-established ones to "plug and play", a system with Principles, Practices and Programs that are duplicable! Duplication is simple to conceive but not always easy to execute. When done correctly, duplication of a powerful system makes large incomes and personal freedoms inevitable. Ask not so much if an action or technique or strategy works; ask instead if the action or technique or strategy is duplicable for success!

21 Ps™

WORLD'S SUREST...FASTEST...SYSTEM FOR MONEY & SUCCESS...MLM CUSTOM GUIDEBOOK

CHAPTER 5
PATTERNING and MODELING: DUPLICATING SUCCESS, THE KEY TO MLM

DUPLICATING THE BELIEFS AND VALUES OF SUCCESSFUL MLM LEADERS

As discussed in Chapter 4 on Power (Personal and External), Beliefs and Value Systems are the foundations to powerful actions, behaviors and optimum results. Successful MLM Leaders have refined their skills and abilities sometimes by trial and error and often through years of valuable experience. Beliefs and values that have been tested and proven as successful in producing empowering strategies and actions are the ones to be patterned after and modeled. The beliefs and values must be universal and demonstrably empowering, as opposed to attributes that might only be possessed by a uniquely gifted or brilliant Leader.

PROGRAM EXERCISE 1
Research and choose a successful MLM Leader (or two) and discover their universal belief and value systems that are empowering and have worked over time and circumstance. List the Leader's beliefs and mind-sets such as how they develop people, or how they overcome hardships, or deal with frustrations or specific challenges to MLM issues, or how they approach their MLM business.

_____

_____

_____

_____

_____

_____

_____

_____

_____

_____

_____

_____

_____

_____

21 Ps™

WORLD'S SUREST...FASTEST...SYSTEM FOR MONEY & SUCCESS...MLM CUSTOM GUIDEBOOK

PATTERNING and MODELING: DUPLICATING SUCCESS, THE KEY TO MLM

DUPLICATING THE SEQUENCE OF STEPS IN A SUCCESSFUL MLM SYSTEM

In every MLM Company, there is a sequence of steps for a new Representative to follow that starts with being first introduced to the business opportunity to ending up being a successful Leader with a large growing organization generating large sales volumes, creating other powerful Leaders (as many as possible) with growing incomes from Team production and ultimately long-term residual income. Successful Teams or at least successful members of a Team have performed effective duplication and are teaching it to their recruits and downline.

PROGRAM EXERCISE 2
What is the proven sequence of steps in a successful Team in your MLM Company? Or your Team (led by your Sponsor or someone very successful in your upline)? Ascertain these steps from your Team and Company Leaders and follow them in detail:

_____

_____

_____

_____

_____

_____

_____

_____

_____

_____

_____

_____

_____

_____

21 Ps™

WORLD'S SUREST...FASTEST...SYSTEM FOR MONEY & SUCCESS...MLM CUSTOM GUIDEBOOK

CHAPTER 5
PATTERNING and MODELING: DUPLICATING SUCCESS, THE KEY TO MLM

APPLYING AND USING THE RIGHT TOOLS, MATERIALS & RESOURCES FOR MLM SUCCESS

Attendant to the sequence of Duplicable Steps above (Introduction / Exposures / Presentations / Meetings / Trainings) are the Tools for Marketing / Prospecting / Communications / Promotions / Business / Accounting / Etc. These Tools are what make Duplication feasible, especially if they are "3rd Party" Tools, meaning that any Representative and Prospect can access them readily such as News Articles, Conference Calls, Webcasts, Websites, Brochures and Special Training Materials (such as this Book).

PROGRAM EXERCISE 3
List your Team's Tools that are used in the Duplicable Steps in your MLM business. Analyze their effectiveness by asking Prospects, other Representatives and your downline and upline. Emphasize the Tool's ease of Duplication that will allow for repeated exposures to the business opportunity to Prospects and Potential Customers. Use the Tools to solidify your MLM Team's duplication efforts.

_____

_____

_____

_____

_____

_____

_____

_____

_____

_____

_____

_____

_____

21 Ps™

WORLD'S SUREST...FASTEST...SYSTEM FOR MONEY & SUCCESS...MLM CUSTOM GUIDEBOOK

DUPLICATING AND MODELING THE "LOOK"/ACTIONS OF TOP MLM LEADERS

Patterning the Belief and Value Systems of a Top MLM Achiever may require deep research or really getting to know the Leader. Another strategy of duplication looks into modeling the Leader's style.

PROGRAM EXERCISE 4
Once again, select a very successful Leader in your MLM Company and learn as much as possible about him or her: any personal background, history in the company or organization, even his or her lifestyle, etc. Describe their "Look" and Actions at Presentations, Meetings and Trainings. Imitation is the sincerest form of flattery as you try to emulate *some* of the Top Performer's style, in addition to their substance which should be the duplicable steps discussed in Program Exercise 2 above.

_____

_____

_____

_____

_____

_____

_____

PROGRAM EXERCISE 5
Describe the ways and means to promote and maintain Duplication for yourself and your Team. What are some of the techniques and strategies to consistently and continuously practice Duplication?

_____

_____

_____

_____

_____

_____

_____

21 Ps™

WORLD'S SUREST...FASTEST...SYSTEM FOR MONEY & SUCCESS...MLM CUSTOM GUIDEBOOK

CHAPTER 5
PATTERNING and MODELING: DUPLICATING SUCCESS, THE KEY TO MLM

REMINDERS / NOTES / EXTRA SPACE FOR EXERCISES:

_____

_____

_____

_____

_____

_____

_____

_____

_____

_____

_____

_____

_____

_____

_____

_____

_____

_____

_____

21 Ps™

WORLD'S SUREST...FASTEST...SYSTEM FOR MONEY & SUCCESS...MLM CUSTOM GUIDEBOOK

SECTION 2:

THE MULTI-LEVEL/NETWORK MARKETING COMPANY'S 5 "Ps"

THIS SECTION IS MAINLY ADDRESSED TO PROSPECTS FOR AN MLM BUSINESS OPPORTUNITY AND POTENTIAL CONSUMERS OF MLM PRODUCTS AND SERVICES.

ACTUAL MLM COMPANIES ARE PORTRAYED AND ANALYZED REGARDING THEIR PROPOSITIONS, THEIR ACTUAL PRODUCTS OR SERVICES, THEIR PEOPLE (ESPECIALLY FOUNDERS AND LEADERS), THEIR PRICING (OF COMPANY PRODUCTS AND SERVICES), AND FINALLY THE MLM COMPANY'S PAY STRUCTURE (THEIR COMPENSATION PLANS) FOR THOSE PROSPECTS CONSIDERING TO JOIN THE BUSINESS OPPORTUNITY.

THIS SECTION IS ALSO VALUABLE FOR NEW OR ESTABLISHED MLM REPRESENTATIVES (DISTRIBUTORS OR ASSOCIATES) FOR BOTH PROSPECTING AND TRAINING. THE PRESENTATION OF ACTUAL MLM COMPANIES ALLOWS THE MLM REPRESENTATIVE TO LEARN ABOUT NETWORK MARKETING IN GENERAL AS WELL AS ALLOW THEM TO PLACE THEIR OWN MLM COMPANY IN CONTEXT OF INDUSTRY PRACTICES AND PROGRAMS.

IF THE MLM REPRESENTATIVE'S COMPANY CAN SHOW LEGITIMACY AND EXCELLENCE AMONG THE COMPETITION AND IF THE MLM INDUSTRY CAN BE REPRESENTED AS HAVING GREAT IN-DEMAND PRODUCTS AND SERVICES, IN ADDITION TO POWERFUL BUSINESS OPPORTUNITIES FOR THOSE SEEKING PERSONAL AND FINANCIAL FREEDOMS, CONSUMERS AND PROSPECTS AND THE PARTICIPATING ECONOMIES AROUND THE WORLD ALL WIN!

Note: The inclusion of MLM Companies and their information (which are sourced from company websites, business journals and trade association publications such as Direct Selling News) are not endorsements or testimonials. The whole purpose of this SECTION is for Customers and Prospects (would-be Representatives) and Representatives themselves to conduct due-diligence and personal verifications of figures, statements and pronouncements.

21 Ps™
WORLD'S SUREST...FASTEST...SYSTEM FOR MONEY & SUCCESS...MLM CUSTOM GUIDEBOOK

BLANK PAGE FOR

SECTION 2

NOTES

21 Ps™

WORLD'S SUREST...FASTEST...SYSTEM FOR MONEY & SUCCESS...MLM CUSTOM GUIDEBOOK

CHAPTER 6
PROPOSITION: CULTURE and WHAT THE COMPANY IS ALL ABOUT

The (MLM) Customer is King and "always right" while the Prospect of an MLM Opportunity can potentially have a royal lifestyle if he or she gets it right in choosing the right MLM Company. Most Prospects become Representatives actually by being "chosen", that is recruited and convinced through presentations and exposures to MLM products and services and opportunities by family, friends or persuasive network-marketers who become the Representative's Sponsor.

This Chapter and the rest of SECTION 3 deal with the process of Customers and Prospects proactively selecting an MLM Company as if they had not been marketed to and recruited. Ideally an MLM Representative should be the one to choose the MLM Company and its Opportunity and Products/Services. However since the process is often reversed, this Section will serve not only the Customers and Prospects who can choose their situations and possible destinies, but also those MLM Representatives who are already in a given MLM Company to be able to *confirm* their "choice" or perhaps elect to find a different MLM Company that is in fact perfect or right for them by judiciously leaving their present MLM Company!

If Customers or Prospects can have full confidence in a specific MLM Company and in Network Marketing in general, they will sell themselves on worthwhile products/services and be most likely convinced of the MLM business opportunity. A Prospect who becomes an official Representative for an MLM Company has to realize that their objective is to successfully and proudly represent the Company for the long-term. A Company whose culture, image and missions are congruent with a Representative (former Prospect) will have a greater chance for quicker and long-lasting success in the MLM business.

The cultures and missions of actual MLM Companies will be depicted in this Chapter. These are the avowed credos and statements of real Companies that serve as examples for Customers and Prospects to examine and compare with other Companies whose products/services they might be considering or whose business opportunities they might be recruited for (if not the example Companies themselves). Mission statements and pronouncements have of course to be proven by a Company's actual behavior and activities that are codified in its Policies and Procedures.

For those already in their "chosen" MLM Companies, Representatives must understand and agree (contractually) with their Company's Policies and Procedures and also ideally be in harmony with the Company's culture and missions. It is important for self-motivation and for prowess in prospecting and presentation that the Representative does in fact know and can articulate his or her Company's culture and missions. The Representative must internalize what the MLM Company is all about as he or she goes about the daily routines of opportunity introductions, prospecting, sales and follow-ups. The fit between the MLM Company and the Representative will determine how motivated, skilled and persevering the Representative will be in the face of any hardships, frustrations and competition.

Customers and Prospects of MLM Opportunities and Products/Services have a universe of choices. An MLM Company's culture and what it is all about are starting points that will attract the most loyal customers and potentially the most motivated and informed Prospects to become achievement-seeking MLM Representatives!

<u>21 Ps</u>™

WORLD'S SUREST...FASTEST...SYSTEM FOR MONEY & SUCCESS...MLM CUSTOM GUIDEBOOK

CHAPTER 6
PROPOSITION: CULTURE and WHAT THE COMPANY IS ALL ABOUT

EXAMPLES OF THE CREDOS AND MISSION STATEMENTS OF ACTUAL MLM COMPANIES:

COMPANY: AMWAY

In many ways Amway is the premier MLM Company in breadth of products/services, size (annually either #1 or #2 in Total Global Revenues), success, reputation and culture. Amway has been the business and legal (regulatory) proving-ground of Network Marketing. Started and still headquartered in Ada, Michigan by MLM pioneers Rich DeVos and Jay Van Andel in 1959 (and now run by scions Doug DeVos and Steve Van Andel), Amway's basic credo has established the standard for MLM:

"Provide direct selling and business opportunities for entrepreneurs in your neighborhood or around the world offering well-known brands. Build a network of support locally, regionally and from the entire global corporation to foster growth, success and community."

COMPANY: AVON PRODUCTS, INC.

Avon is another iconic MLM Company that was ranked #1 in Revenues in 2010 ($10.9 Billion). Even older that Amway and before the advent of MLM, Avon's well-known brands in cosmetics, fragrances and toiletries (as well as newer lines in fashion jewelry, apparel and toys) are "network-marketed" by 6.5 Million Distributors. Andrea Jung is CEO at the Avon headquarters in New York, New York.

"'Avon Ladies' are part of global popular culture: Independent Sales Representatives who use direct selling (network marketing) to market and sell desirable cosmetic and fashion products. Avon empowers women's causes such as Breast Cancer Health Care, Domestic Violence Prevention, Women's Training and Literacy, the Environmental Movement, and Global Disaster Relief through the Avon Foundation and through special product sales. (Although dominated by women, there are also thousands of 'Avon Gentlemen'.)"

<u>Notes for Customers/Prospects considering the products/services & opportunities of above MLM Companies:</u>

_____

_____

_____

_____

_____

_____

_____

21 Ps™

WORLD'S SUREST...FASTEST...SYSTEM FOR MONEY & SUCCESS...MLM CUSTOM GUIDEBOOK

EXAMPLES OF THE CREDOS AND MISSION STATEMENTS OF ACTUAL MLM COMPANIES:
(Continued)

COMPANY: MONAVIE LLC

An example of a relatively new MLM Company, MonaVie was founded in 2005 and still run by Dallin A. Larsen from its headquarters in South Jordan, Utah. MonaVie is a "nutritional beverage" company with a product line formulated from the acai berry and other "nutrient-dense" fruits. MonaVie's 2010 revenues totaled $855 million (Inc. Magazine) generated by some 1 million Distributors in the United States, Canada, Australia, Brazil, New Zealand, Singapore, Japan, Israel, and the United Kingdom.

"MonaVie invests millions of dollars in scientific studies and is dedicated to unlocking, sharing, and protecting the most unique, health-giving resources the Earth has to offer. Partnering with renowned research institutions and universities as well as leading authorities on health and nutrition, newly enhanced MonaVie products help fight the damaging effects of oxidative stress while supporting your overall health."

COMPANY: HERBALIFE LTD.

Founded in 1980, headquartered in Los Angeles, CA, Herbalife's CEO is Michael O. Johnson. Herbalife is the 5th largest MLM Company in revenues ($2.7 Billion in 2010) with 2.1 Million Distributors marketing products including nutritional supplements, weight-management and personal-care products. Starting with its classic mobile advertisements of "Lose weight now, ask me how?", Herbalife proclaims:

"We are a global nutrition company that has helped people pursue a healthy, active life since 1980. Our nutrition, weight-management and personal care products are available exclusively through our more than 2.1 million independent Distributors in 75 countries. We support the Herbalife Family Foundation (HFF) and its Casa Herbalife program to help bring good nutrition to children in need. We also sponsor world-class athletes, teams and events around the globe, including the LA Galaxy and FC Barcelona soccer clubs, as well as champions in more than 15 other sports. Our Mission is to change people's lives by providing the best business opportunity in direct selling and the best nutrition and weight-management products in the world."

Notes for Customers/Prospects considering the products/services & opportunities of above MLM Companies:

_____

_____

_____

_____

_____

21 Ps™

WORLD'S SUREST...FASTEST...SYSTEM FOR MONEY & SUCCESS...MLM CUSTOM GUIDEBOOK

CHAPTER 6
PROPOSITION: CULTURE and WHAT THE COMPANY IS ALL ABOUT

EXAMPLES OF THE CREDOS AND MISSION STATEMENTS OF ACTUAL MLM COMPANIES:
(Continued)

COMPANY: NU SKIN ENTERPRISES, INC.

Nu Skin is a billion dollar + MLM Company (ranked #10 in 2010 with revenues of $1.5 Billion). Headquartered in Provo, Utah, Nu Skin was founded in 1984 and is headed by CEO Truman Hunt. Nu Skin's 800,000 Distributors are in 48 international markets network-marketing cosmetics, toiletries and fragrances and more than 200 products through three distinct brands: Nu Skin, Pharmanex and Big Planet. Nu Skin is heavily invested in Community Development, Sponsorships, its Nu Skin Force for Good Foundation and various Projects including Nourish the Children (NTC) projects:

"We begin the next 25 years with great momentum. At a time when increasing numbers of people are seeking economic security, our strategy is to provide a focused, innovative, and compelling business opportunity, with particular emphasis on our anti-aging product platform and distributor compensation. As we usher in the next 25 years, we'll continue to be a beacon of innovation and integrity, setting the standard for others to follow as we demonstrate our difference through our people, product, opportunity, and culture."

COMPANY: ORIFLAME COSMETICS S.A.

Oriflame is an example of a non-U.S. Company (founded in 1967 in Sweden and headquartered in Luxembourg with still no U.S. marketing presence) that is experiencing tremendous growth in MLM as it operates in 62 countries (including Mexico and Central and South America) and is the market leader in more than half of its product line of cosmetics, fragrances and personal-care, skin-care, hair-care and wellness products. Oriflame earned $2.2 Billion in revenues in 2010 through its 3.5 million Reps.

"The Oriflame culture gives each person the freedom to set their own targets, income and working hours. It is a culture that is based on respect for and belief in others. We have given millions of people the opportunity to change their lives for the better – an opportunity that many have taken to achieve their dreams. We have given people in Russia, Europe, Asia, South America and Africa the opportunity to start their own business, often in countries where the freedom to do business was discouraged or restricted to a self-appointed elite. In this way, Oriflame has helped tear down walls. We built the first cosmetics factory in Warsaw after the fall of the Berlin Wall."

Notes for Customers/Prospects considering the products/services & opportunities of above MLM Companies:

_____

_____

_____

_____

_____

21 Ps™

WORLD'S SUREST...FASTEST...SYSTEM FOR MONEY & SUCCESS...MLM CUSTOM GUIDEBOOK

EXAMPLES OF THE CREDOS AND MISSION STATEMENTS OF ACTUAL MLM COMPANIES:
(Continued)

COMPANY: TUPPERWARE BRANDS CORP.

Tupperware is another iconic MLM Company founded in 1946 by Earl Silas Tupper, headquartered in Orlando, Florida (Chairman and CEO Rick Goings) whose 2010 revenues of $2.3 Billion was 7th best in MLM. Tupperware with 2.6 million Representatives in nearly 100 countries sells innovative design-centric preparation, storage and serving products for the kitchen and home, as well as beauty and personal-care items.

"Changing Lives...One at a Time:
Tupperware Brands is passionate about changing lives and everything we do is channeled to express that passion to everyone of the 2 million independent sales force members. We are also passionate about the quality and integrity of our products. The need to offer consistent quality and to act with integrity is also a critical component of our relationship with our independent sales force, employees, and shareholders. We meet their expectations through a stringent internal code of conduct and through our strong corporate governance policies, which support our core values of integrity and trust."

COMPANY: THE PAMPERED CHEF LTD.

Pampered Chef is a half-billion dollar revenue MLM Company ($500 Million in 2010), founded in 1980, headquartered in Addison, Illinois and run by Marla Gootschalk, CEO. Owned by Warren Buffet's Berkshire Hathaway since 2002, Pampered Chef offers more than 300 gourmet kitchen tools, cookware, cookbooks and foodstuffs through its 60,000 Distributors-Consultants.

"Offer business and social opportunities for the cooking aficionado (the talented or enthusiastic cook or cook-to-be) and those who love food (who doesn't?) to sell desirable products and the concept of preparing delicious quality meals economically and quickly. The Pampered Chef "Party Plan" is a time-tested direct selling approach (proven successful by Tupperware, etc.): using the products, a Pampered Chef Representative does a Cooking Show demonstration at a home. The Consultant cooks food and guests get to eat during the show!

Notes for Customers/Prospects considering the products/services & opportunities of above MLM Companies:

_____

_____

_____

_____

_____

21 Ps™

WORLD'S SUREST...FASTEST...SYSTEM FOR MONEY & SUCCESS...MLM CUSTOM GUIDEBOOK

CHAPTER 6
PROPOSITION: CULTURE and WHAT THE COMPANY IS ALL ABOUT

PRACTICE EXERCISE 1A:
(For the Representative in an existing MLM Company)
Following the examples of statements and pronouncements of the actual companies in this Chapter, brainstorm and summarize in 1, 2 or 3 sentences your MLM Company's Culture and "What the Company is all About". (If your Company is one of the actual examples in this Chapter, describe actual real-life illustrations of the Company's Proposition in your daily business practices or in how you represent the Company personally.)

_____

_____

_____

_____

_____

PRACTICE EXERCISE 1B:
(For Customers or Prospects of an MLM Company)
If you are being recruited by a Representative of an MLM Company, ask about or learn its Proposition (Culture and "What the Company is all About"). Do you like what you hear or discover? Are the MLM Company's principles or avowed philosophy reflected in the Representatives and its Products and Services? Could you possibly join this MLM Company or even buy its products/services?

_____

_____

_____

_____

_____

_____

_____

21 Ps™

CHAPTER 7
PRODUCT or SERVICE: UNIQUE or SPECIAL and MARKETABLE?

Network Marketing has evolved into a preeminent global business and distribution model (over $125 Billion in revenues world-wide in 2010 according to the Direct Selling Association) that covers just about every product, service and industry. Once again a proactive Customer or Prospect (actively seeking a business opportunity) has the full spectrum of choices to suit needs, taste and affinity.

Customers can find unique products and services that may be purchased at "wholesale" just by becoming an official Representative without necessarily working toward a business venture. Because mass advertising is minimized or streamlined, and "middlemen" and similar distribution layers are removed with products going more or less direct from manufacturer to end-user, products and services may be less expensive for the consumer. Or someone (the efficient MLM Rep between the producer and the consumer) can be an integral part of and profit from the role as an efficient marketer and distributor of the product or service.

MLM Companies have in fact been pioneers in the introduction of products and services that have eventually become mainstream, from phone cards to vitamins to anti-aging cosmetics to water filters. If a Prospect is interested in the business concept and believes in the viability of Network Marketing, he or she can explore the multitude of products and services that can be "network marketed". The value of being exposed to a particular Company may be the ability to explore various companies that are in industries that a Prospect has a true ability or passionate interest. If someone will go into a business to expend effort, time and resources, it might as well be an area of appeal and ideally excitement!

This Chapter will portray various MLM Companies in such industries as Nutrition, Wellness, Weight Management, Legal Services, Real Estate, Insurance, Green Products, Telecommunications, Housewares and Energy as well as MLM Companies with wide consumer product lines for Representatives (Distributors or Associates) to use, market and sell.

To maximize business profitability and sustainability, Prospects must consider not just their attraction to a product or service, but also issues of marketability (size, demographics and purchasing power), quality of the product or service, and whether the product or service is a "durable" or a "consumable" all of which would have effects on profitability and income.

The legitimacy and long-term success of an MLM Company will rest on its products and services. While the paradigm of Multi-Level Marketing is a proven business success, no amount of hype and outbalanced focus on any "business opportunity" can overcome inferior products or services that face competition from not just other MLM Companies (who may eventually copy successful "exclusive" products) but also competition from the general market place.

Consumers are the general winners in the proliferation of products and services and how they are produced, marketed and distributed. Prospects who will pursue the dream of potential business success and thus become MLM Company Representatives will find the optimal intersection of their passions and interests meeting products and services that are ideal for network marketing: products and services that require demonstration, explanation and personal use and testimony of its great features and benefits!

21 Ps™

WORLD'S SUREST...FASTEST...SYSTEM FOR MONEY & SUCCESS...MLM CUSTOM GUIDEBOOK

CHAPTER 7
PRODUCT OR SERVICE: UNIQUE or SPECIAL and MARKETABLE?

COMPANY: ACN, Founded 1993 in United States (2010 Revenues of $553 Million)

PRODUCTS OR SERVICES: Telecommunications Services (Local and long distance phone service, digital phone service with video, Internet, wireless, satellite TV), home security, computer support and energy

INDUSTRY: Telecommunications, Home and Business Services

MARKET CONDITIONS: Excellent prospects for growth in both industrialized and developing countries.

COMPANY: TELECOM PLUS, Founded 1998 in United Kingdom (2010 Revenues of $600 Million)

PRODUCTS OR SERVICES: Landline phones, broadband, mobile phones, gas, electricity

INDUSTRY: Telecommunications and Energy

MARKET CONDITIONS: Even if only in one market (The U.K.), Telecom Plus has greater revenues than longer-established ACN above. It also has less than half the employees as ACN (500 vs. 1300). Is it better managed or does it have better products? And how successful are the companies' respective Distributors? A lesson in researching and considering similar MLM Companies.

COMPANY: NATURA; Founded 1969 in Brazil (2010 Revenues of $3.2 Billion)

PRODUCTS OR SERVICES: Cosmetics, Perfume; Skin Care; Hair Care; Solar Filters

INDUSTRY: Cosmetics and Personal Care

MARKET CONDITIONS: In 6 Latin American countries (Argentina, Brazil, Chile, Colombia, Mexico and Peru) and France, Natura is ranked #3 world-wide in revenues among MLM Companies. Adapting to its markets well, Natura has surpassed Avon in sales in Brazil since 2006: has very popular products such as home bikini waxes, a focused image of being eco-friendly, and uses "ordinary" women instead of models in ads.

Notes for Customers/Prospects considering the products/services & opportunities of above MLM Companies:

_____

_____

_____

_____

PRODUCT OR SERVICE: UNIQUE or SPECIAL and MARKETABLE?

COMPANY: OMNILIFE; Founded in 1992 in Mexico (2010 Revenues of $750 Million)

PRODUCTS OR SERVICES: Nutritional supplements, weight-management, beauty products, beverages, cosmetics and perfumes

INDUSTRY: Nutritional Supplements, Beauty and Personal Care

MARKET CONDITIONS: Another large MLM Company with a strong market presence in 23 countries in South America, North and Central America as well as Asia and Europe. Omnilife is a powerful entrepreneurial force in Mexico and Latin America with its 5 Million Representatives and 3,500 employees.

COMPANY: YANBAL INTERNATIONAL; Founded in 1967 in Peru (2010 Revenues of $600 Million)

PRODUCTS OR SERVICES: Skin care, cosmetics, personal-care products, fragrances and jewelry

INDUSTRY: Cosmetics and Personal-Care

MARKET CONDITIONS: A long established MLM Company that utilizes the party-plan system to market its products (350,000 Representative-Beauty Consultants). Popular in South America.

COMPANY: USANA HEALTH SCIENCES INC.; Founded in 1992 in U.S. (2010 Revenues of $517 Million)

PRODUCTS OR SERVICES: Nutritional supplements; weight management and personal care products

INDUSTRY: Nutritional Supplements and Personal Care

MARKET CONDITIONS: A long-established MLM Company that despite strong competition and some controversy and litigation over its products and management has become a half-billion dollar per year revenue company with products marketed in the U.S. Canada, Australia, New Zealand, United Kingdom, Netherlands, Japan, Hong Kong, Taiwan, Korea, Singapore, Mexico, Malaysia, The Philippines, and China.

<u>**Notes for Customers/Prospects considering the products/services & opportunities of above MLM Companies:**</u>

_____

_____

_____

_____

_____

21 Ps™

WORLD'S SUREST...FASTEST...SYSTEM FOR MONEY & SUCCESS...MLM CUSTOM GUIDEBOOK

CHAPTER 7
PRODUCT OR SERVICE: UNIQUE or SPECIAL and MARKETABLE?

COMPANY: PARTYLITE (BLYTH); Founded in 1973 in U.S. (2010 Revenues of $545 Million)

PRODUCTS OR SERVICES: Candles, candle warmers, flameless fragrance, home accents, personal care and food products

INDUSTRY: Specialty Household and Personal Care Products

MARKET CONDITIONS: PartyLite, owned by conglomerate Blyth, is the world's largest direct seller of candles, fragrance accessories and home ambiance products. PartyLite independent Consultants or Distributors demonstrate and sell PartyLite collections at home parties in 16 countries.

COMPANY: THIRTY-ONE GIFTS; Founded in 2004 in United States (2010 Revenues of $100 Million)

PRODUCTS OR SERVICES: Handbags, women's accessories and personalized gifts

INDUSTRY: Women's Bags and Accessories

MARKET CONDITIONS: A mid-sized MLM Company that has grown steadily and centered on a Christian theme as Thirty-One refers to Proverbs 31 of the Bible which describes the ideal and virtuous Christian woman.

COMPANY: KIRBY COMPANY; Founded in 1914 in United States; (2010 Revenues of $100 Million)

PRODUCTS OR SERVICES: Vacuum cleaners and household cleaning products

INDUSTRY: Household Products

MARKET CONDITIONS: Kirby Company serves as an example of an MLM Company (a subsidiary of the Scott Fetzer Company which in turn is part of Warren Buffet's Berkshire Hathaway) with only one product which is a limitation that has been overcome with the MLM model (person-to-person and unilevel pay plan).

Notes for Customers/Prospects considering the products/services & opportunities of above MLM Companies:

_____

_____

_____

_____

21 Ps™

WORLD'S SUREST...FASTEST...SYSTEM FOR MONEY & SUCCESS...MLM CUSTOM GUIDEBOOK

CHAPTER 7
PRODUCT OR SERVICE: UNIQUE or SPECIAL and MARKETABLE?

COMPANY: WORLD FINANCIAL GROUP; Founded in 1992 in U.S. (2010 Revenues of $80 Million)

PRODUCTS OR SERVICES: Life Insurance, Annuities, Mutual Funds and various Financial Products

INDUSTRY: Life Insurance and Financial Products

MARKET CONDITIONS: World Financial Group (WFG) evolved from troubled World Marketing Alliance (WMA). WFG was purchased and given its name by Dutch financial giant Aegon (2010 Revenues of over $50 Billion). WFG markets through network marketing in the U.S. and Canada.

COMPANY: KELLER WILLIAMS REALTY INC.; Founded in 1983 U.S. (2010 Revenues of $120 Million)

PRODUCTS OR SERVICES: Real Estate Brokerage and Loan Services

INDUSTRY: Real Estate

MARKET CONDITIONS: Keller Williams is the third largest residential real estate company in the United States whose 75,000 real estate agents are actually franchisees and technically MLM Representatives who operate in more than 650 market centers (offices) across the United States and Canada.

COMPANY: PREPAID LEGAL SERVICES, INC.; Founded in 1972 in U.S. (2010 Revenues of $454 Million)

PRODUCTS OR SERVICES: Legal services and identity theft restoration

INDUSTRY: Legal Services

MARKET CONDITIONS: Pre-Paid Legal is an example of another essential service that is "network marketed". Pre-Paid Legal works with some 50 independent provider-law-firms across the United States and Canada. Though faced with its own legal battles over income representation and its own stock repurchasing, Pre-Paid Legal has continued to grow and illustrates network marketing's success as a business model.

Notes for Customers/Prospects considering the products/services & opportunities of above MLM Companies:

_____

_____

_____

_____

21 Ps™

WORLD'S SUREST...FASTEST...SYSTEM FOR MONEY & SUCCESS...MLM CUSTOM GUIDEBOOK

CHAPTER 7
PRODUCT OR SERVICE: UNIQUE or SPECIAL and MARKETABLE?

-FOR THE MLM REPRESENTATIVE-
PROGRAM EXERCISE 1
What are your MLM Company's Products and/or Services? Research and describe the market conditions for your products (whether the market is growing, what the competition is like, and if you can in fact identify your market).

(If your MLM Company is already featured in this Chapter, describe and give examples of how you or your family (friends, associates) or actual Customers have benefitted from the product or service.)

_____

_____

_____

_____

_____

_____

_____

_____

_____

_____

_____

_____

_____

_____

_____

_____

_____

_____

21 Ps™
WORLD'S SUREST...FASTEST...SYSTEM FOR MONEY & SUCCESS...MLM CUSTOM GUIDEBOOK

CHAPTER 8
PEOPLE: FOUNDERS, LEADERS, MANAGERS, SPONSORS and REPS

"People" are *not* a company's most valuable assets, the "*Right* People" are! Many MLM Companies have been founded by individuals with the "right stuff" to go on and become legends and icons of free enterprise.

Pioneers such as Rich DeVos and Jay Van Andel, Mary Kay Ash, Earl Silas Tupper, Dr. Forrest Shaklee, Mark Hughes, Jorge Madrigal, Rick Williams and Mabel Baker have set the benchmarks of greatness for many new exemplars of the current generation including Greg Provenzano, Frank Vandersloot, Magnus Brännström, Heidi and Orville Thompson, Rob Snyder and Andrea Jung.

The notable founders and originators of the enterprises that have become great Network Marketing Companies have created the cultures and missions that have reproduced (in characteristic MLM form) the necessary great people to sustain success in the management and operations of companies that have reached prominence in industry after industry.

The competitive and growing MLM Companies are characterized by Leaders, Managers, Sponsors and Representatives who excel in administration, financial management, marketing, technology, customer service and distribution. At the level of the Representative who conducts his or her MLM business activities on a daily basis, reliability, smooth operations, quality control, ethics and company support are merely standard expectations. The Prospect of the MLM Company's opportunity will be attracted by "excellence" and lofty company promises that must then be delivered when the Prospect becomes an MLM Business Associate.

Since duplication of behaviors and practices are such key components of MLM business success, the duplication of Leaders is a critical issue. It might be foolhardy and unrealistic for Representatives to make their standards of success that of the Company superstars. What must be duplicated are the beliefs, values, principles, missions *and* daily actions of the successful MLM practitioners in the company. Naturally, Representatives will be more likely to follow and duplicate Leaders who are not just financially prosperous but also have integrity, competence and admirable values.

For the MLM Company Prospect and the existing MLM Company Representative, the fundamental considerations to join or stay with a Company are the characteristics of those who are prominent examples in their routine activities, including top management and employees of the head office, but most especially their direct Sponsors and upline who will be mentors, trainers and supporters. Do the "people" of an MLM Company embody its principles and missions? Not just during the stages of prospecting and recruitment but in transactions, meetings, trainings and normal interactions?

This Chapter will feature a few of the past and present champions of some large and medium-sized MLM Companies. The stories of the "greats" are legendary as a means to show Prospects the MLM industry's evolution in the world of business and enterprise; their heroic backgrounds are also meant to motivate and inspire Representatives to aspire to their own individual greatness and unique abilities to succeed in their own way!

21 Ps™

WORLD'S SUREST...FASTEST...SYSTEM FOR MONEY & SUCCESS...MLM CUSTOM GUIDEBOOK

CHAPTER 8
PEOPLE: FOUNDERS, LEADERS, MANAGERS, SPONSORS and REPS

MARY KAY ASH, FOUNDER; MARY KAY INC.

After being in direct selling for already 25 years and facing the limits of being a woman entrepreneur, Mary Kay Ash founded Beauty by Mary Kay in 1963 with $5,000 in savings and the help of her then 20-year old son, Richard.

Mary Kay Ash became an icon in American business and now Mary Kay Inc., a privately held company has revenues of $2.4 Billion (2007 figures) with an Independent Sales force of 1.8 million worldwide (as of 2008) in over 35 countries. A proclaimed member of the 5 o'clock Club (as in getting up at 5am for work), Ms. Ash stated: "The success of Mary Kay Inc. is much, much deeper than just dollars and cents and buildings and assets. The real success of our Company is measured to me in the lives that have been touched and given hope."

FORREST C. SHAKLEE, FOUNDER; SHAKLEE CORPORATION

Dr. Forrest C. Shaklee was an early 20th Century wellness pioneer, a San Francisco chiropractor, who created "Shaklee's Vitalized Minerals" in 1915. In 1956, Dr. Shaklee founded the Shaklee Corporation with his two sons to manufacture nutritional supplements as the concept of vitamins and supplement was starting to go mainstream in health and culture.

Using the one-time relatively unknown multi-level marketing business model, Shaklee's products began to spread as he was one of the first to market health-oriented products, not just his nutritional supplements but also organic and biodegradable cleaning chemicals. Well before any trends or movements, Dr. Shaklee continually focused on concepts of "natural" and "environmentally friendly" in his marketing campaigns.

PROGRAM EXERCISE 1:
If you are a Prospect specifically interested in Mary Kay Inc. or Shaklee Corporation and are being recruited by your would-be Sponsor, have her (or him) fill out her/his brief biography here. (Otherwise as either a Prospect or an existing Representative of a specific company not in this Chapter, go to the last page (page 62) of this Chapter for your Sponsor (to-be) to fill out their brief biography especially at it relates to MLM.):

_____

_____

_____

_____

_____

_____

21 Ps™

WORLD'S SUREST...FASTEST...SYSTEM FOR MONEY & SUCCESS...MLM CUSTOM GUIDEBOOK

ROB SNYDER, FOUNDER; IGNITE INC.

Rob Snyder was a young (40-something) very successful private equity investor when he seized upon an opportunity. In 2004, Snyder co-founded and became Chairman of Stream Energy in Dallas, TX. As befitting a Leader who seeks answers and does not claim infallibility, Rob admits he had no idea that the state of Texas deregulated its electricity market. But he was smart enough to discover that a number of companies were offering electricity at 20 percent less than what he was personally paying for the service.

Rob Snyder was also then visionary enough to launch Ignite in 2005 as an MLM business that would meet the needs of consumers and entrepreneurs in the electricity and natural gas industries that had been changed with deregulation. Starting in its first year of 2005 with $70 million in gross revenues in its one market of Texas, Ignite reached 2010 revenues of $900 million and foresees revenues by the end of 2011 to hit 1 billion dollars with services already expanded in Georgia, Pennsylvania and Maryland.

ALBERT J. AMATUZIO, FOUNDER; AMSOIL SYNTHETIC LUBRICANTS & CHEMICALS

Albert Amatuzio was obsessed with high-end performance of man and machine as a jet fighter pilot for the U.S. Air Force. Amatuzio achieved the rank of Lieutenant Colonel upon retirement. In 1972 Albert founded Amsoil that eventually became the first synthetic motor oil to meet American Petroleum Institute (API) standards.

Amsoil is aimed at enthusiastic motor vehicle owners and knowledgeable customers, formulating clean and high performance synthetic motor oils that need to be replaced up to only once a year or up to 25,000 miles. Amsoil is actually a hybrid retail and network marketing opportunity for "Dealers", Preferred & Catalog Customers, and Commercial Accounts in North America and beyond. For Founder Amatuzio the MLM business means to "promote AMSOIL products with facts, not wild claims...a straightforward way we promote ourselves...very important to maintain a good reputation, both personally and professionally..."

PROGRAM EXERCISE 2:
If you are a Prospect specifically interested in Ignite Inc. or Amsoil Synthetics and are being recruited by your would-be Sponsor, have her (or him) fill out her/his brief biography here. (Otherwise as either a Prospect or an existing Representative of a specific company not in this Chapter, go to the last page (page 62) of this Chapter for your Sponsor (to-be) to fill out their brief biography especially at it relates to MLM.):

_____

_____

_____

_____

_____

_____

21 Ps™

WORLD'S SUREST...FASTEST...SYSTEM FOR MONEY & SUCCESS...MLM CUSTOM GUIDEBOOK

CHAPTER 8
PEOPLE: FOUNDERS, LEADERS, MANAGERS, SPONSORS and REPS

BERNARD CHUA, FOUNDER & CEO; ORGANO GOLD COFFEE

Bernard ("Bernie") Chua became a direct marketing legend as he built a 500,000 Member Direct Sales organization in the Philippines and won "Direct Sales Representative of the Year" for 3 years in a row in Asia with Gano Excel. Chua founded Organo Gold Coffee in 2008 with the belief that "since people drink so much coffee anyway, people won't have to change their habits if they also want to be healthy."

Organo Gold claims to base its products (including tea and chocolate) on "100% Certified Organic Ganoderma Lucidium, perhaps the most amazing botanical on Earth." Bernie Chua confidently expects his MLM Representatives to be succeeding "in front of five powerful industries": 1) Health & Wellness; 2) Weight Loss; 3) Home Based Business; 4) The Internet & 5) Coffee (the 2nd largest traded commodity).

FRANK VANDERSLOOT, FOUNDER & CEO; MELALEUCA INC.

Frank Vandersloot became CEO of Oil of Melaleuca in 1985 and inherited a disaster. He had to start over and start almost worse than zero as half of the company's Representatives left. The first month's sales were $75,000 and growth extremely slow in the first three to four years as the Company was still trying to communicate its revamped business model and mission to the public. After the new Melaleuca's fifth year, the Company made the "Inc. 500". In 2010 revenues were $750 million.

Frank Vandersloot states, "the best advice I can give is that bad news doesn't always equal bad results. If the original company, Oil of Melaleuca, had been even a marginal success then we wouldn't have been tempted to plow ahead. It's just because Oil of Melaleuca was such a disaster that Melaleuca has become a success. If something isn't working, don't be afraid to plow it under and start over."

PROGRAM EXERCISE 3:
If you are a Prospect specifically interested in Organo Gold Coffee or Maleleuca and are being recruited by your would-be Sponsor, have her (or him) fill out her/his brief biography here. (Otherwise as either a Prospect or an existing Representative of a specific company not in this Chapter, go to the last page (page 62) of this Chapter for your Sponsor (to-be) to fill out their brief biography especially at it relates to MLM.):

_____

_____

_____

_____

_____

_____

21 Ps™

WORLD'S SUREST...FASTEST...SYSTEM FOR MONEY & SUCCESS...MLM CUSTOM GUIDEBOOK

CHAPTER 8
PEOPLE: FOUNDERS, LEADERS MANAGERS, SPONSORS and REPS

RHONDA ANDERSON, FOUNDER & CEO; CREATIVE MEMORIES

Rhonda Anderson was a mother and housewife in Montana with her own social circle of other mothers and families. Rhonda's passion was preserving photos and stories in keepsake albums, her family's tradition. Rhonda was astonished to learn that her fellow-moms didn't know about special albums and instead kept their photos stuffed in drawers, various boxes, and under the bed.

In 1987 Rhonda Anderson founded Creative Memories with a vision that one day millions of people would be celebrating family memories and telling their unique stories in photo-safe (acid-free paper) albums. In July 1987, Creative Memories' first Consultant signed on. In 2010 Creative Memories generated revenues of $113 million with tens of thousands of Representative-Consultants worldwide who make a difference in the way individuals and families remember, celebrate, and create connections.

VICTOR K. KIAM, EMERITUS FOUNDER; LIA SOPHIA

Victor was an American high-achiever who attended Yale, the Sorbonne and Harvard Business School. He excelled in the corporate world with Lever Brothers and Playtex, making his fortune as President and CEO of Remington Products, which he famously purchased after his wife bought him his first electric shaver and became a spokesperson with "I liked the shaver so much, I bought the company."

Lia Sophia Fashion Jewelry and Accessories evolved from Lady Remington led by Victor Kiam's son, Victor "Tory" Kiam III. The MLM opportunity Lia Sophia, named after two of Victor Kiam's granddaughters, is centered on the principles of family, entrepreneurship and fashionable lifestyles. Lia Sophia earned revenues of $100 million in 2010.

PROGRAM EXERCISE 4:
If you are a Prospect specifically interested in Creative Memories or Lia Sophia and are being recruited by your would-be Sponsor, have her (or him) fill out her/his brief biography here. (Otherwise as either a Prospect or an existing Representative of a specific company not in this Chapter, go to the last page (page 62) of this Chapter for your Sponsor (to-be) to fill out their brief biography especially at it relates to MLM.):

_____

_____

_____

_____

_____

_____

21 Ps™

WORLD'S SUREST...FASTEST...SYSTEM FOR MONEY & SUCCESS...MLM CUSTOM GUIDEBOOK

CHAPTER 8
PEOPLE: FOUNDERS, LEADERS, MANAGERS, SPONSORS and REPS

-FOR EXISTING MLM REPRESENTATIVES-
PROGRAM EXERCISE 5:
It is important for a Representative (or Prospect) to gain confidence in an MLM Company's owners, founders, investors and leaders. If you already know of your Company's Founders and top management from this Chapter or from published company information, describe a leader in your own team or organization. Feature a new leader, especially one with a powerful story of overcoming hardships or obstacles or someone who through dedication, commitment and smart work made it "big".

_____

_____

_____

_____

_____

_____

_____

-FOR EXISTING MLM REPRESENTATIVES OR PROSPECTS-
PROGRAM EXERCISE 6:
Discover and describe your direct Sponsor's (Recruiter's) brief biography here (or have them fill out the info). Remember a sponsor (eventually you) is ideally a figure one can proudly emulate and fully duplicate for MLM success!

_____

_____

_____

_____

_____

_____

_____

21 Ps™

WORLD'S SUREST...FASTEST...SYSTEM FOR MONEY & SUCCESS...MLM CUSTOM GUIDEBOOK

CHAPTER 9
PRICING: WHAT ARE THE COSTS, INCENTIVES and THE COMPETITION?

The Pricing of MLM products and services affect competition among companies (MLM and non-MLM), whether the products and services are regarded as consumables or luxuries or exclusive, and leads to the measurement of profits for an MLM Company and how fairly those profits are distributed to MLM Representatives.

There are often retail prices (for Customers) and wholesale prices (for the resale or consumption by MLM Representatives). Buying "wholesale" is many times the motivation for customers and prospects to sign up to become an MLM Representative. Still the intrinsic worth of products and services are what will produce loyal and repeat customers. There have been instances when MLM Companies have suffered credibility when their products may have been overpriced from overhype and unsubstantiated claims of product benefits that ultimately led to Company failures, especially those companies that are centered on a main product (from some special herb or fruit or botanical): the proverbial "$40 bottle of juice".

Competition has a direct influence on pricing and how sustainable an MLM's product line will be. When products are seen as commodities such as household and basic personal-care items, competition from outside the MLM Companies will be fierce. The customer must be convinced of an MLM's product's superiority or bottom-line value (such as a higher formula concentration or if a product is environmentally friendly) in the midst of so many products and services available, especially in the developed countries.

If a product is in fact exclusive or developed from an MLM Company's intensive and costly Research and Development that has created highly-demanded features and benefits, pricing may then be less vulnerable to competition but still subject to the desires of consumers and the ability of competitors to copy or improve or substitute for the "exclusive" product. Branding also has its benefits as demonstrated by the successful MLM Companies that have evolved the brands of their products and services in targeted markets over time. Especially in the areas of cosmetics and women's merchandise, the very successful MLM Companies such as Avon, Natura, Amway and Mary Kay (with many other smaller companies following suit) have developed world-class brands to compete with any other global brands.

The large MLM Companies have developed wide product lines that allow their Representatives to offer variety to their customers and potential prospects (for the business opportunity itself). In general MLM Companies should have flexibility in their profit margins since the network marketing distribution model can be made more efficient and because mass advertising can theoretically be supplanted by word-of-mouth. There have been times when MLM Companies have been able to enter a new industry because national monopolies in such areas as telecommunications or energy have been eliminated or adjusted by regulation and deregulation.

The ideal scenario for everyone involved in network marketing (the Customer, the Prospect, the Representative and the MLM Company) is when efficiencies, quality and loyalty all come together so that products and services are priced competitively to generate values for the buyer, seller and producer. If an outstanding product or invaluable service benefits a consumer greatly even at "retail" price, the potential is enhanced for a customer to not just spread the word but also become an official MLM Company Representative to spur profits for all!

21 Ps™

WORLD'S SUREST...FASTEST...SYSTEM FOR MONEY & SUCCESS...MLM CUSTOM GUIDEBOOK

CHAPTER 9
PRICING: WHAT ARE THE COSTS, INCENTIVES and THE COMPETITION?

AMWAY RETAIL PRICE (in U.S. Dollars) EXAMPLES:

Nutrilite 450 g Protein Powder: $30.75
See Spray Cleaner (1 liter): $7.80
Atmosphere Air Purifier: $859.99

Artistry Time Defiance Skin Care System: $166.95
Magic Foam Carpet Cleaner (21 oz.): $8.40
eSpring Water Purifier System: $922.79

If you are a Customer considering Amway, list any other products you are interested in and their prices:

_____

_____

_____

If you are a Prospect considering the Amway business opportunity, what are the available product *incentives* and what are the *"wholesale"* prices of the above products?

_____

_____

_____

WORLD VENTURES RETAIL PRICE (in U.S. Dollars) EXAMPLES:

"Dream Trip" prices:
Jamaica vacation at the Grand Lido Braco (1 week for 2 adults) = $890 vs. Travelocity price of $1050
Cabo San Lucas trip to Riu Palace (5 days for 2 adults) = $758 vs. Travelocity price of $950

If you are a Customer considering World Ventures, list any "Dream Trips" you are interested in & their prices:

_____

_____

_____

If you are a Prospect considering the World Ventures business opportunity, what are the available product **incentives** and what are the *"wholesale"* prices of the above products?

_____

_____

_____

21 Ps™

WORLD'S SUREST...FASTEST...SYSTEM FOR MONEY & SUCCESS...MLM CUSTOM GUIDEBOOK

CHAPTER 9
PRICING: WHAT ARE THE COSTS, INCENTIVES and THE COMPETITION?

AVON RETAIL PRICE (in U.S. Dollars) EXAMPLES:

Anew Ultimate Age Defying System: $28.00   Reese in Bloom Fragrance: $34.00
Avon Enhanced Renewing Lotion, 6.8 oz.: $19.50   MagiX Finish Liquid Foundations SPF 10: $11.00

If you are a Customer considering Avon, list any other products you are interested in and their prices:

_____

_____

_____

If you are a Prospect considering the Avon business opportunity, what are the available product **incentives** and what are the *"wholesale"* prices of the above products?

_____

_____

_____

PAMPERED CHEF RETAIL PRICE (in U.S. Dollars) EXAMPLES:

Roasting Pan with Rack & Meat Lifters: $153.00   11" Square Grill Pan & Grill Press: $299.00
Reversible Bamboo Carving Board & Carving Set: $184.50   Large 18" x 15" Bamboo Platter: $31.95
Stoneware Plates and Pans: $16 to $70   Dining Table Pieces: $12 to $160 (16-pc set)

If you are a Customer considering Pampered Chef, list any other products you are interested in and their prices:

_____

_____

_____

If you are a Prospect considering the Pampered Chef business opportunity, what are the available product **incentives** and what are the *"wholesale"* prices of the above products?

_____

_____

_____

21 Ps™

WORLD'S SUREST...FASTEST...SYSTEM FOR MONEY & SUCCESS...MLM CUSTOM GUIDEBOOK

CHAPTER 9
PRICING: WHAT ARE THE COSTS, INCENTIVES and THE COMPETITION?

<u>MARY KAY</u> RETAIL PRICE (in U.S. Dollars) EXAMPLES:

TimeWise Age-Fighting Moisturizer: $22
Satin Lips Set: $18
TimeWise 3-in-1 Cleanser: $18

Mary Kay Ultimate Mascara (Black): $15
Oil-Free Eye Makeup Remover: $15
Satin Hands Pampering Set: $34 per set

If you are a Customer considering <u>Mary Kay</u>, list any other products you are interested in and their prices:

_____

_____

_____

If you are a Prospect considering the <u>Mary Kay</u> business opportunity, what are the available product *incentives* and what are the *"wholesale"* prices of the above products?

_____

_____

_____

<u>AMSOIL</u> RETAIL PRICE (in U.S. Dollars) EXAMPLES:

Signature 0W-30 100 Synthetic Motor Oil (1 Quart): $10.50
SAE 10W-30 100% Synthetic Motor Oil (1 Quart): $9.15

AMSOIL Synthetic Nano-fiber Oil Filter: $14.35
AMSOIL SDF88 Oil Filter (Power Diesel): $23.60

If you are a Customer considering <u>Amsoil</u>, list any other products you are interested in and their prices:

_____

_____

_____

If you are a Prospect considering the <u>Amsoil</u> business opportunity, what are the available product *incentives* and what are the *"wholesale"* prices of the above products?

_____

_____

_____

21 Ps™

WORLD'S SUREST...FASTEST...SYSTEM FOR MONEY & SUCCESS...MLM CUSTOM GUIDEBOOK

CHAPTER 9
PRICING: WHAT ARE THE COSTS, INCENTIVES and THE COMPETITION?

TUPPERWARE RETAIL PRICE (in U.S. Dollars) EXAMPLES:

"Go-anywhere serving & storage collection" (9-Pc): $30.00   Medium Eco Water Bottles (4): $34.00
Floresta Serving Dishes: $29.50   Complete Kitchen Prep Set: $99.00
Tupperware Revolutionary Microwave SmartSteamer: $139.00   Quick Shake (Mixer) Container: $13.00

If you are a Customer considering Tupperware, list any other products you are interested in and their prices:

_____

_____

_____

If you are a Prospect considering the Tupperware business opportunity, what are the available product *incentives* and what are the *"wholesale"* prices of the above products?

_____

_____

_____

ORGANO GOLD COFFEE RETAIL PRICE (in U.S. Dollars) EXAMPLES:

Gourmet Black Coffee: $4.95   Gourmet Mocha Coffee: $8.95   Gourmet Latte Coffee: $5.95
Gourmet Hot Chocolate: $8.95   Gourmet Organic Green Tea: $6.95   King of Coffee: $9.95

If you are a Customer considering Organo Gold, list any other products you are interested in and their prices:

_____

_____

_____

If you are a Prospect considering the Organo Gold Coffee business opportunity, what are the available product *incentives* and what are the *"wholesale"* prices of the above products?

_____

_____

_____

21 Ps™

WORLD'S SUREST...FASTEST...SYSTEM FOR MONEY & SUCCESS...MLM CUSTOM GUIDEBOOK

CHAPTER 9
PRICING: WHAT ARE THE COSTS, INCENTIVES and THE COMPETITION?

-FOR CUSTOMERS, PROSPECTS & MLM REPRESENTATIVES-
PROGRAM EXERCISE 1
For MLM Companies not featured in this Chapter, list products you are interested in or are selling and their prices:

_____

_____

_____

_____

_____

-FOR PROSPECTS & MLM REPRESENTATIVES-
PROGRAM EXERCISE 2
For MLM Companies not featured in this Chapter, describe specific *incentives*, prizes and bonuses offered (and what it takes to get them):

_____

_____

_____

_____

_____

-FOR PROSPECTS & MLM REPRESENTATIVES-
PROGRAM EXERCISE 3
For any MLM Company you are interested in or involved with, describe any other pricing-related aspects such as monthly *"auto-ship"* policies and amounts, and also mention new product introductions, if any:

_____

_____

_____

_____

_____

21 Ps™

WORLD'S SUREST...FASTEST...SYSTEM FOR MONEY & SUCCESS...MLM CUSTOM GUIDEBOOK

CHAPTER 10
PAY and INCOME: COMPENSATION PLANS and BUSINESS INVESTMENTS

Assuming a Customer and a Prospect are interested or just wondering about the income potential of an MLM Company, this Chapter focuses on Compensation Plans that at times may seem overly complicated or technical. Four of the most basic types of Pay or Compensation Plans used by almost all MLM Companies will be discussed.

For a Representative who is just starting out in an MLM Company, a way to judge his or her Company's fairness and sustainability is to measure how much its profits are distributed to all Representatives. Ideally 40% to 55% of an MLM's profits from its products and up to 80% of its profits from service offerings should be paid to its Representatives.

The differences among Companies should be not be the overall percentage range but whether profits are distributed in a balanced way to assist new Representatives earn some income in the first 90 days or so (to help in retaining the prospects who have just started in business) and the "little guy" who may just be working part-time, and also the seasoned Representative who needs to be rewarded for staying with the Company and having recruited a wide line of Representatives.

To receive income from an MLM Company requires some minimum of personal sales to remain an active Representative. The large incomes will of course come from generating personal sales and more importantly group sales from the organization that a Representative develops with time and effort as he or she goes up in rank or position.

Prospects and Representatives may not totally understand all the elements of a Compensation Plan. This Chapter will allow basic knowledge of Pay Plans that will be best learned with actual practice and when the actual checks are calculated and paid! Facility with Pay Plans will also make overall duplication of the MLM success activities easier as Representatives can teach Prospects who will be able to teach or present to others when they themselves become new Representatives.

The key questions for Prospects considering the business opportunity of an MLM Company regarding the critical Pay Plan are whether it is fair, whether there are exciting incentives for those who join and produce results, whether there might be special bonuses beyond commissions such as free cars and vacations available, and of course whether the Pay structure is realistic and achievable.

The MLM opportunity is ultimately a business that for the serious prospect will also involve business expenses and investments to create momentum and growth. While the investments are relatively modest such as product purchases or investments in training, self-development and personal marketing, they are necessary for eventual success. Because the Representative is plugged into a system that has economies of scale, any Representative investment is low-risk with potentially very high returns.

If the MLM Company is reputable with a culture and mission that are admirable and evident, if people in the MLM Company are honest, competent and passionate, and if the MLM products or services are excellent, competitively-priced and marketable, then a serious Prospect can make a proactive decision and be able to take a leap of confidence and sign up to become a Representative in the MLM Company and its Pay Plan.

21 Ps™

WORLD'S SUREST...FASTEST...SYSTEM FOR MONEY & SUCCESS...MLM CUSTOM GUIDEBOOK

CHAPTER 10
PAY and INCOME: COMPENSATION PLANS and BUSINESS INVESTMENTS

<u>STAIRSTEP BREAKAWAY</u> COMPENSATION PLAN
(Some version used by about 60% of all MLM Companies):

RANKS AND EARNINGS PERCENTAGE RATES:

National
Director

Regional
Director

Manager

Executive   Supervisor

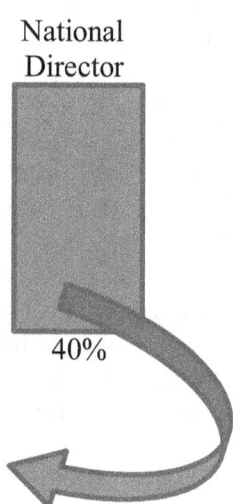

20%   25%   30%   35%   40%

Generational Bonus % Paid on Breakaway Legs:

BREAKAWAY:

Generations 1: 5%

Generations 2: 5%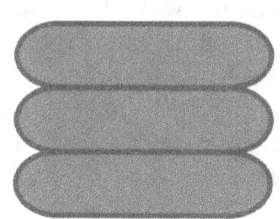

Generations 3: 5%

FEATURES OF THE STAIRSTEP BREAKAWAY PLAN:

No limit on how many one person can recruit.

No limit on how many people one can have at first levels (top line: people directly recruited).

Each personal recruit (at first level) forms a new line (or leg) which can potentially break away.

One can earn commission on personal group (one's top line and the people they recruit).

Commissions are earned by meeting a monthly personal and group sales target.

Note the commission percentage pay rates at each stair step rank above: From Executive to Directors.

Note that the bonus commission percentage pay rates are for an entire generation of a breakaway leg. (As long as one stays ahead by a higher rank.)

21 Ps™

WORLD'S SUREST...FASTEST...SYSTEM FOR MONEY & SUCCESS...MLM CUSTOM GUIDEBOOK

FORCED MATRIX COMPENSATION PLAN
(Used in some version by some 12% of all MLM Companies):

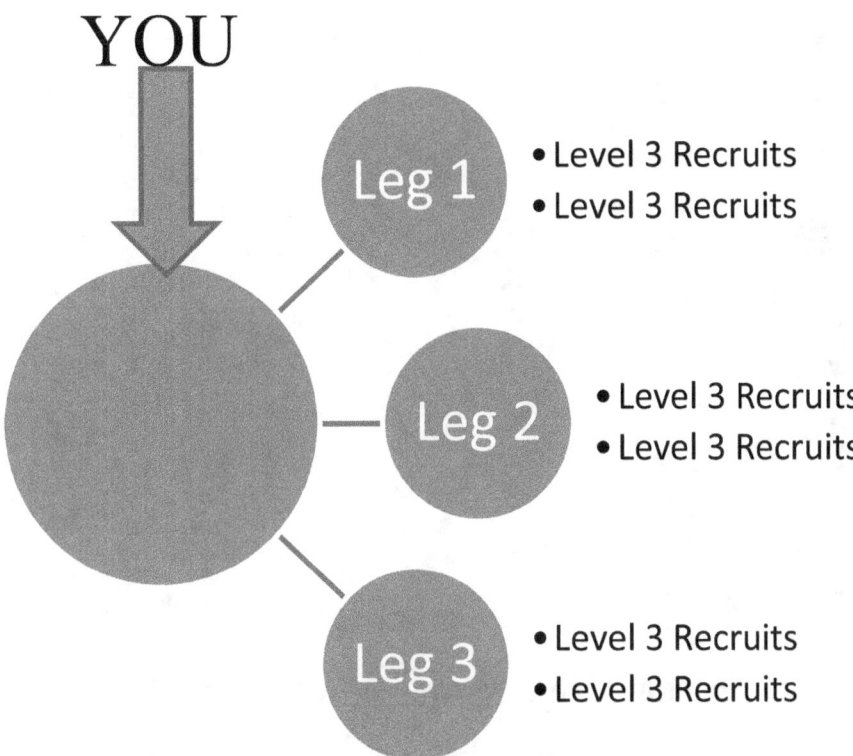

FEATURES OF FORCED MATRIX COMPENSATION PLAN:

Number of people personally recruited across the Top Level (known as Level 2 below you) is ***limited***.

People recruited by your direct recruits are known as Level 3.

Depending on the Company, the number of downline levels (depth) may also be limited.

Any people you directly recruit over your limit will drop a level (termed spillover).

There are both advocates and critics of the Forced Matrix Compensation Plan. Those in favor like the plan because open spots in the hierarchy will be filled by spillover to the benefit of less-senior or less-active Representatives. Opponents of the plan argue that non-industrious Representatives get dependent on the organization to fill open space under them with little or no effort. This Plan is used popularly with Internet marketing and affiliate programs.

CHAPTER 10
PAY and INCOME: COMPENSATION PLANS and BUSINESS INVESTMENTS

UNILEVEL OR UNIGEN COMPENSATION PLAN
(Used by about 18% of all MLM Companies):

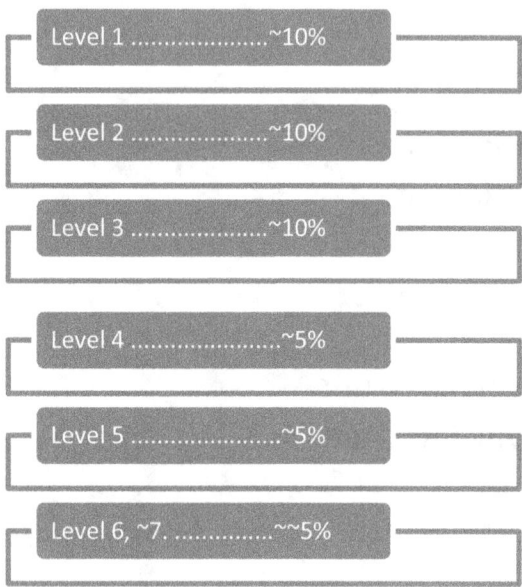

Level 1 ....~10%

Level 2 ....~10%

Level 3 ....~10%

Level 4 ....~5%

Level 5 ....~5%

Level 6, ~7. ....~~5%

FEATURES OF THE UNILEVEL OR UNIGEN COMPENSATION PLAN:

Similar to the Stairstep Breakaway, the Unilevel or Unigen Compensation pays commissions on personal and breakaway groups.

The Unilevel Plan is wide ("democratic" or "socialistic") in that money is shared with everyone in the organization which might limit large individual incomes unless there are enhanced features to increase income such as generational bonuses.

If someone is a personal Leader/Sponsor of a very deep and large organization, he or she can earn substantial generational bonus income with Companies that offer such an incentive.

Representatives (often called Associates or Members) are encouraged to sell to a customer base that can be personally serviced at "retail".

Representatives (Associates or Members) generally earn a higher commission on direct personal recruits than through other types of Compensation Plans.

With the Unilevel or Unigen Compensation Plan, it is possible to earn as much income from the bottom level of a sales organization as from the top level, especially if commission percentages are equal for each level. Companies may vary and pay one or more levels higher percentages according to policy and design.

21 Ps™

WORLD'S SUREST...FASTEST...SYSTEM FOR MONEY & SUCCESS...MLM CUSTOM GUIDEBOOK

BINARY COMPENSATION PLAN
(Used by less than 10% of all MLM Companies):

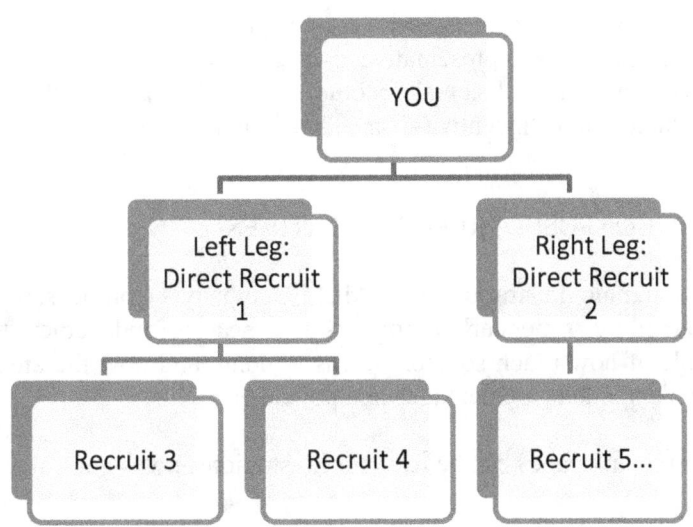

FEATURES OF THE BINARY COMPENSATION PLAN:

You can only recruit two (thus the term binary) people or legs as your First Levels.

Any additional direct recruits are forced to Second Levels, etc.

Commissions are paid on the sales of the weaker of the two Legs. Some Companies allow for the carrying forward of unpaid sales.

Pays commissions quickly (often on a weekly basis) and encourages people to work together closely because commissions are paid on creating specific amounts of sales revenue.

Recruitment is placed at a premium which sometimes makes motivation for focusing on products and personal/leadership development weaker.

Note: Some companies are allowing Representatives to form a second matrix.

Fewer and fewer MLM Companies are using this "simple compensation plan", except for some foreign companies that are trying the network-marketing model for existing product lines in their domestic markets.

CHAPTER 10
PAY and INCOME: COMPENSATION PLANS and BUSINESS INVESTMENTS

REMINDERS AND BOTTOM-LINES

The bottom-line to making income in a legitimate MLM Company with marketable products or services is to be compensated fairly for hard (smart) work in offering business opportunities to new Prospects and for generating personal and group sales.

Since this has been in many respects the most technical Chapter of the Book, what would be made simple and satisfactory for Prospects and (new) Representatives is to be shown an actual real-world illustration of an MLM Company's Compensation Plan and actual income earned through the Plan. Such terms as "personal volume" and "group volume" and "incentives" and "position/rank commission percentages" will come to life with actual examples.

-FOR PROSPECTS AND (NEW OR CONFUSED) REPRESENTATIVES-
PROGRAM EXERCISE 1
Ask your Sponsor or Recruiter for a graphic illustration of the MLM Company's Compensation Plan. (While it is illegal to show "large" checks earned by "superstar" performers as a means of inducement to a "speculative" business opportunity, a real example of how much someone earns a month and how the amount is calculated would confirm a Compensation Plan's numbers, percentages and policies.)

The rest of this page and the next two blank pages can be used for illustrations, notes and calculations.

_____

_____

_____

_____

_____

_____

_____

_____

_____

_____

_____

_____

21 Ps™

WORLD'S SUREST...FASTEST...SYSTEM FOR MONEY & SUCCESS...MLM CUSTOM GUIDEBOOK

CHAPTER 10
PAY and INCOME: COMPENSATION PLANS and BUSINESS INVESTMENTS

BLANK PAGE FOR <u>MLM COMPANY</u> COMPENSATION PLANS

<u>Notes / Illustrations / Calculations</u>

21 Ps™

WORLD'S SUREST...FASTEST...SYSTEM FOR MONEY & SUCCESS...MLM CUSTOM GUIDEBOOK

CHAPTER 10
PAY and INCOME: COMPENSATION PLANS and BUSINESS INVESTMENTS

BLANK PAGE FOR <u>MLM COMPANY</u> COMPENSATION PLANS

<u>Notes / Illustrations / Calculations</u>

SECTION 3

THE MULTI-LEVEL/NETWORK MARKETING TEAM'S 5 "Ps"

THIS IS THE 3RD MAIN AND FINAL SECTION OF THE "21 Ps" SYSTEM FOR MLM OR NETWORK MARKETING MONEY AND SUCCESS. THE MLM REPRESENTATIVE OR THE PROSPECT WHO HAS JOINED THE BUSINESS NEEDS TO MASTER THE "5 Ps" OF THE MLM TEAM.

THIS 3RD SECTION IS ABOUT THE MASTERY OF SPECIFIC INDUSTRY SKILLS THAT ARE SET ON THE FOUNDATION OF PERSONAL ABILITIES AND POWERS DEVELOPED IN SECTION 1 AND THE CONVICTION CREATED FROM KNOWING OR CONFIRMING THE RIGHT COMPANY TO JOIN IN SECTION 2.

THE MLM TEAM IS THE VEHICLE AND THE STRUCTURE USED FOR THE INDIVIDUAL MLM REPRESENTATIVE'S ACCOMPLISHMENTS. THE SUM OF THE PARTS AND THE MLM SYSTEM ARE MAXIMIZED IN ALL THE AREAS AND STAGES FOR SURVIVAL, SUSTAINABILITY AND HIGH ACHIEVEMENT. IN THE END, BUILDING A GREAT (MLM) TEAM IS THE ONLY WAY TO ATTAIN INCREDIBLE AND LASTING INCOME!

THE 5 CHAPTERS THAT FOLLOW COVER PROSPECTING (PARTNERING); PRESENTATIONS; PROCESS; PROMOTIONS; AND FINALLY THE PINNACLE OF SUCCESS!

21 Ps™
WORLD'S SUREST...FASTEST...SYSTEM FOR MONEY & SUCCESS...MLM CUSTOM GUIDEBOOK

BLANK PAGE FOR

SECTION 3

NOTES

21 Ps™

WORLD'S SUREST...FASTEST...SYSTEM FOR MONEY & SUCCESS...MLM CUSTOM GUIDEBOOK

CHAPTER 11
PROSPECTING (PARTNERING): ATTITUDES, SKILLS and LISTS/VENUES

Prospecting may be the greatest "mechanical" and "skill" variable of MLM success for both new and established (if still not accomplished) Representatives. Once someone has decided to join a business opportunity and has some degree of mastery and continual commitment to self-improvement in areas such as Purpose, Perseverance and Personal Power, the mechanics and the realities of actually finding Customers and Prospects to the new MLM venture are critical and ongoing issues.

Deficiencies in Prospecting skills have a direct bearing on getting both the quantity and quality of Prospects and Customers. A new Representative can be as motivated and enthusiastic as possible but the inability to get new recruits or only finding recruits who are not as inspired or ambitious as required will eventually discourage even the most determined MLM novice or veteran. The encouraging news is that prospecting skills can be learned and applied and can immediately improve results that reverse setbacks and start a *virtuous* cycle.

Prospecting must be viewed in a fundamentally different way from the "old school" ways of selling that in the past centered on manipulation, "hard selling", and viewing the Prospect as someone who is different from the "Prospector" (the "seller") with opposing or different agendas or interests. Prospects must be viewed as Partners; Selling must be approached as Consulting, Sharing and Problem-Solving; Products or Services to sell must be considered as something beyond the thing itself and instead be deemed as offerings that lead to opportunity, freedoms and dreams.

Since prospecting means dealing with people both art and (social) science are involved. The powerful social nature of Multi-Level/Network Marketing is reflected in the infinite and creative ways of prospecting that have proven to work for the high-income and long-successful MLM practitioners. Not surprisingly, the value and power of the Team concept confirm the social aspects of the MLM business. Only by building great and powerful teams can individual Representatives realize their greatest potential for long-lasting high incomes and satisfaction. Prospecting is part of a Team's activities.

The social aspects of prospecting are corroborated by the Principles, Practices and Programs of system duplication discussed in detail in Chapter 5 ("Patterning and Modeling: Duplicating Success, the Key to MLM"). Only by creating a team that practices Duplication can there be the attainment of excellent or enormous incomes for individuals who apply the system dutifully. When prospecting skills are refined and consistently employed to produce a large number of potential Business Leaders, a Representative can better qualify Prospects to develop as Leaders, those who will replicate and duplicate a system and be themselves excellently skilled Prospectors in an ever expanding successful organization.

This Chapter will explore the Attitudes required for successful Prospecting as well as the concrete Skills and the specific Tools and Techniques required to get Customers and the ideal Business-Builders that make the smart and consistent efforts pay off. Prospecting is the basis for practicing the rest of the 5 Ps of the MLM Team's quest for survival, greatness and longevity. Great MLM practitioners must be generated from Prospects who will eventually become new Leaders. The ideal objective of Prospecting is the discovery of individuals who will become influential Leaders and Teachers of a system for Money and Success!

21 Ps™

WORLD'S SUREST...FASTEST...SYSTEM FOR MONEY & SUCCESS...MLM CUSTOM GUIDEBOOK

CHAPTER 11
PROSPECTING (PARTNERING): ATTITUDES, SKILLS and LISTS/VENUES

ATTITUDE 1
"NATURAL" PROSPECTING

In the spirit of "consultative selling" where instead of manipulative or traditional selling (buyer must be "closed"), Prospecting should be a possibility to share, listen, ask questions, understand and ultimately solve problems when appropriate or when prompted. Prospects will be led to decide on their own that the MLM Company's products or services and the business opportunity are right for them *now*. Thus timing and persistent exposure is important so that the Customer/Prospect will be attracted to the visible, trusted and focused MLM Representative. This type of Prospect will have the greatest potential for success and MLM leadership and system duplication because he or she is self-motivated and probably open to coaching and mentoring to optimize the opportunity that they he or she has concluded is a great fit.

ATTITUDE 2
YOU ARE DOING CUSTOMERS AND PROSPECTS A SERVICE

You the MLM Representative are doing the Customer/Prospect a favor and not the other way around! If the recruiting Representative has done the due diligence of Company research and has begun to master and commits to self-improvement, then he or she will have confidence in the products or services and the MLM business opportunity itself. It would be a benefit for a Prospect to be able to take advantage of the same opportunity and it will *not* be a matter of difficulty for the Representative to convey the opportunity's ultimate benefits to a potentially receptive Prospect.

ATTITUDE 3
ALMOST EVERYONE IS A PROSPECT

Prospects are everywhere. Since the MLM opportunity is sound and potentially life-changing for the better, most eligible people are in fact candidates for the products or services. With the attitude that everyone can be a prospect, a Representative is ever ready to expose or introduce the products and the opportunity.

ATTITUDE 4

EVEN IF EVERYONE IS A PROSPECT, YOU ARE IDEALLY LOOKING FOR THE RIGHT ONES

The right Prospects are the ones looking for an opportunity at the optimal time in their lives. Since you seek to develop Leaders and Business Builders who can duplicate systems of actions and successful results, prospecting will be less stressful and be more efficiently done.

ATTITUDE 5

YOU ARE MARKETING NOT NECESSARILY PRODUCTS BUT DREAMS AND FREEDOMS

When prospecting, conceive of the big picture beyond products or services and the past or present. You are offering Customers and Prospects the opportunity to pursue their own ambitions, Purposes, personal dreams and individual freedoms. Prospecting thus becomes lofty and less mundane.

Other general Attitudes are also valuable for successful Prospecting (Partnering) including Confidence, Enthusiasm, Mental Toughness and the internal mindsets developed in SECTION 1 of this Book: Purpose, Productivity and Perseverance.

21 Ps™

WORLD'S SUREST...FASTEST...SYSTEM FOR MONEY & SUCCESS...MLM CUSTOM GUIDEBOOK

SKILL 1
BE (MORE) SOCIABLE

Prospecting comes in the course of common and everyday interactions. Being social animals, humans gravitate to those who are more gregarious, friendly and likeable. A shy person or introvert will not necessarily be bad at prospecting if he or she can be just more open and communicative in their own ways and styles. A more relaxed demeanor, a simple smile, a genuine "hello" all project a basic sociability that can lead to more self-confidence and courage to apply the tools and techniques than can be learned.

SKILL 2
BE VISIBLE

Related to sociability is the skill of visibility, again in terms and styles suitable to the personality of the "Prospector". Visibility might start with just showing up at more public venues, gatherings or events. Being proud and expressive of who you are (an MLM Representative with the appropriate Attitudes discussed above) is a baseline posture for visibility. The visible prospecting Representative has the materials, knowledge, answers to concerns, and promotional tools that can be readily available when the prized Prospect shows up or approached.

SKILL 3
BE EVER READY

When the Prospect, through effort, circumstance or fortune is finally available, the MLM Representative must be ready with her recruitment methods, tools and materials. Brochures, business cards, testimonials, CDs, Tapes, DVDs and Books must be ready to be shown or handed-out. An immediate supply of marketing or the quick ability to access promotional resources such as websites, conference calls, etc. will mark the MLM Representative as a professional who is also modeling behavior to a Prospect who might soon become a member of the MLM team!

SKILL 4
BE TIMELY

Successful Prospecting is of course a matter of consistent and repeated efforts. For many people, it may not be the right time to buy a product or service or start a business opportunity. If Prospects are in fact receptive to the benefits of product or service or opportunity and the recruiting Representative is perceived as competent, trustworthy and likeable, then it is really just a matter of time before the Prospect is ready to buy or join a team. The "Prospector" needs to be professional, persistent and ready *when* the Prospect is ready.

SKILL 5
BE A DUPLICABLE PRODUCT AND MODEL

When an MLM Representative demonstrates all of the above skills (and the Attitudes that project his or her statements, behavior and actions), he or she is modeling for Prospects those attributes that will make prospecting truly pay off. The very characteristics that get Prospects to start an MLM business opportunity are the very traits that will also work for the newly signed-up to get the best kind of Prospects of their own: those who will follow a system, those who will commit to become a trainable team of Leaders!

<u>21 Ps</u>™

WORLD'S SUREST...FASTEST...SYSTEM FOR MONEY & SUCCESS...MLM CUSTOM GUIDEBOOK

CHAPTER 11
PROSPECTING (PARTNERING): ATTITUDES, SKILLS and LISTS/VENUES

LIST 1
YOUR "WARM" and "WARMER" MARKET PROSPECTS

Friends and Family constitute your warm market. Many people naturally start here to look for Prospects for Products/Services and the MLM business opportunity. However some others do not feel comfortable approaching this market for different reasons such as being uneasy about being a "prophet in the house" or if a Representative has tried other MLM opportunities with this market unsuccessfully. Ultimately this market can be won over by just being straight and truthful (as required because of past MLM attempts) and when the Representative has had some measure of success with their "cold" markets. Friends and family can eventually be the most stalwart supporters and perhaps co-business partners if the business opportunity is in fact the breakthrough that has finally happened for the at-long-last flourishing MLM practitioner.

LIST 2
YOUR REFERRAL PROSPECTS

This should be a special list category because referrals should be consistently cultivated in every kind of Prospecting. For those people not interested, getting appropriate referrals from them makes the prospecting effort fruitful despite the *current* response of "No". Referrals can become closer to the status of a warm or "warmer" market when they are recommended by a person who is now seen as a common friend or associate.

LIST 3
YOUR SOCIAL ACTIVITIES PROSPECTS

As part of a "cold" market, acquaintances and *virtual* strangers have to be a consistent portion of a prospecting plan that keeps the stream of Prospects flowing. Speaking of virtual, as will be discussed in the next section on Prospecting Techniques, *virtual* strangers now become Friends because of the enormous power of social networking (pioneered and amplified by Facebook, MySpace, YouTube and Twitter). Affinity groups such as common professions and common interests are also sources of "Social Activities" Prospects.

LIST 4
YOUR "NEW PEOPLE AS YOU MEET" PROSPECTS

The Attitudes of "Natural Prospecting" and the way Prospects are considered in the mind of the MLM Representative that underlie the Skills of Sociability, Visibility, Readiness, Timeliness and Duplicability require a List of any new people met on a daily or regular basis. "Everyone is a Prospect!" At any time!

LIST 5
YOUR CREATIVE MARKETING PROSPECTS

Since in many ways, the whole world is full of Prospects, it is just a matter of creativity, style, preference, time and budget for an MLM Representative to conceive and execute a Prospecting Plan and its ensuing Lists. You should consult with your Sponsors and upline for advice and guidance, and to make sure that a particular Prospecting Plan and its marketing or advertising method meets Company policies and guidelines. Special Tools 4 outlines more plans and methods of "Creative Marketing". (See Page 157.)

21 Ps™

WORLD'S SUREST...FASTEST...SYSTEM FOR MONEY & SUCCESS...MLM CUSTOM GUIDEBOOK

CHAPTER 11
PROSPECTING (PARTNERING): ATTITUDES, SKILLS and LISTS/VENUES

VENUE 1
INTERNET SOCIAL NETWORKING

Prospects can be naturally developed in the internet social networking circles of an MLM Representative. Of course even if you had 1000 "Friends" on Facebook or 10,000 Followers on Twitter, it doesn't mean that all in your circle or group will become Customers, much less join you in the MLM business opportunity. It does mean that your identity is expressed and consistent even as you engage and display personal and sometimes frivolous or fun activities on the social networking site. You can still portray your trustworthiness, your competence and likeability that are the marks of successful Prospectors offline.

VENUE 2
PRIVATE PARTIES and CELEBRATIONS

Back in the real world, private parties with families and friends are often events of relaxation and celebration. As the excited or "hard-core" MLM Representative "lives and breathes" the business and prospecting, inevitably the question or discussion of "what do you do?" comes up. The serious MLM Practitioner is who he or she is even in informal situations. Parties and celebrations presuppose that you are known, liked and "real". Your behavior, overt or implicit will show other persons that you (the MLM guy or gal) are happy, legitimate and successful in what you do.

VENUE 3
PUBLIC GATHERINGS and EVENTS

Similarly in public venues where again the questions of "who you are" and "what you do" surface, your actions and appearance will speak volumes of your MLM status. No matter your stage or success level in your MLM business, the people talked to, interacted with and engaged will be potentially attracted by what your opportunity represents. You must be ready with a business card or perhaps a brochure and any promotional materials or at answers (and prepared scripts) to the questions of any interested latent Prospects.

VENUE 4
SPECIAL NOTES ON INTERNET COMMUNICATIONS: POSTING, TWEETING, EMAILING

In first or preliminary marketing/prospecting communications, it is important to NOT oversell or even try to sell at all. Recognize that you have great products/services and a lucrative business opportunity. But people, from virtual strangers to the new Facebook Friend or Twitter Follower, need to perceive value and benefits in your offerings. Create legitimacy and community first and sales will follow naturally.

VENUE 5
SPECIAL NOTES ON TELEPHONE and TEXTING! TECHNIQUES

In the necessary telephone conversations (or texts!) with the newly interested Prospect or the curious Friend who is intrigued by your value offerings online or in person, you need to have explicit objectives. Your aim is to get the Prospect to the next step in your duplicable MLM success system. You must ask brief but probing questions of interest and from the Prospect's answers gauge interest and whether it is appropriate to invite him or her to the next step of either more formal information (such as a CD or tape or book) or a Presentation or Appointment for a possible sign up, the subject of Chapter 12.

21 Ps™
WORLD'S SUREST...FASTEST...SYSTEM FOR MONEY & SUCCESS...MLM CUSTOM GUIDEBOOK

CHAPTER 11
PROSPECTING (PARTNERING): ATTITUDES, SKILLS and LISTS/VENUES

SPECIAL NOTES
-Consistently work on Special Tools 2 (The Prospecting-Partnering Database/Special Lists, pages 135-148)-
Include below your MLM Team's Systematic Prospecting Techniques;
Make Notes here of the various Techniques outlined in Special Tools 4 (Creative Marketing) that appeal to your
personality and style. Assess their effectiveness or incorporate them into your regular Prospecting Activities.

_____

_____

_____

_____

_____

_____

_____

_____

_____

_____

_____

_____

_____

_____

_____

_____

21 Ps™

WORLD'S SUREST...FASTEST...SYSTEM FOR MONEY & SUCCESS...MLM CUSTOM GUIDEBOOK

CHAPTER 12
PRESENTATIONS, APPOINTMENTS & MORE REFINEMENTS OF MLM SYSTEM

The objective of Prospecting is the chance to make persuasive Presentations and consultation Appointments where Prospects will be led to decide for themselves that the MLM opportunity is best for them. Since the ultimate sign-up for the opportunity by the Prospect may take more than one Presentation and Appointment or other exposures, more creative refinements and applications of the MLM System (that includes duplicable Prospecting and continuous self-improvement) are required.

Just as Prospecting involves Attitudes and Skills, fruitful Presentations and Appointments also necessitate the proper approaches and techniques. At this stage of the MLM Process (systematically outlined in detail in the next Chapter), competence and experience are keys. Typically Presentations are done by successful and seasoned Sponsor-Representatives who will start the modeling of the proper actions, behaviors and skills for untested Representatives to learn. Appointments are initially done with the Sponsor accompanying the new Representative in person or via a telephone conference call.

Presentations and Appointments require the nuances of communications that will allow the MLM practitioner to connect the Company's products and opportunity to the Prospect's problems, needs and desires. A thorough knowledge of what the Company offers is essential for someone conducting a Presentation or Appointment. Yet the Prospect must not be inundated with information. The MLM practitioner must somehow probe and discover who the Prospect really is in terms of their current circumstances, their motivations to start a business and whether there is in fact a fit between the opportunity and the potential business partner.

Since communications are critical in Presentations and Appointments, both intellect and emotions are involved. The Prospect's head and heart are both considering the MLM opportunity. At this stage of the MLM recruitment (and training) process, showing all the technicalities of the Compensation Plan or any intricacies of the product or service is not as important as connecting the offerings to what the Prospect really wants. Is the Prospect looking to improve her life? Is the Prospect "stuck" at his job or current business? Is the Prospect in desperate need of additional income? Does the Prospect have hidden dreams and unrealized ambitions?

With all Presentations and Appointments in front of potential Customers and Partners, the MLM Company's attributes are on display, as are the Sponsors, Representatives and indirectly Company personnel and Leaders. From the standpoint of the new Representative, mastering the skills and techniques of Presentations and Appointments is part of the entire MLM process.

Mastery requires practice, practice and more practice. The quality of "performance" in presentations and appointments will improve with time and repetition. In partnership with the Sponsor, the newly minted Representative will eventually have the experience, skills and courage to venture out on their own. The unproven Representative does not have to become a polished public speaker or be slick with scripts and statistics and figures of the Compensation Plan. The new MLM practitioner must only become knowledgeable, competent, trustworthy and caring with his or her own genuine style that can inspire themselves and their Prospects to action with their own dreams and desires!

The rest of this Chapter will discuss the basics and essential qualities of powerful Presentations, and the elements of effective Appointments which ideally center on answering a Prospect's questions and objections that might lead to possible problem-solving that is the MLM Company's products and opportunity. In the end, great products and services and the business opportunity to market and sell them will ideally find the right Prospects to partner with the sponsoring Representative and the supporting Company. Professional presentations and consultative appointments are the openings to make Prospects future Business-Builders.

21 Ps™

WORLD'S SUREST...FASTEST...SYSTEM FOR MONEY & SUCCESS...MLM CUSTOM GUIDEBOOK

CHAPTER 12
PRESENTATIONS, APPOINTMENTS & MORE REFINEMENTS OF MLM SYSTEM

BASIC ELEMENTS OF A PRESENTATION
(AT A GROUP MEETING AT A HOME OR AT A HOTEL)

(1) INTRODUCTION

At the start of the Presentation *everyone* should be introduced if possible (unless there are more than 25 or so total people including guests). This is part of the critical element of Recognition for everyone involved from even successful Sponsors to new Representatives *and* Guests who if they indeed become Representatives will realize the importance of duplicating acknowledgment. People consistently cite the *lack* of recognition (being respected and appreciated are sometimes rated as more important than money) as one of biggest factors to dissatisfaction at the workplace and beyond. Introductions can be as brief as stating name, occupation and reason for coming or any *brief* comments.

(2) BRIEF SYNOPSIS OF COMPANY & PRODUCTS (IDEALLY 15 MINUTES OR LESS)

This is an overview of the MLM industry in general, and summary details of the Company and its main Products or Services. It is important to stress what specific ***benefits*** there are for Prospects for the stated features and qualities of the Company. Extremely detailed information, especially of Products, should be minimized. All presentations must always and foremost be about what is important for Prospects' needs, circumstances and aspirations.

(3) "DREAM BUILDING" (FINDING PURPOSES, MOTIVATIONS AND INSPIRATIONS)

Termed "dream building" by many trainers and sponsors, this part of the Presentation continues the theme of being Prospect-Centered. Recall the Exercises on "Purpose" and "Goals: Where and When" in the first Chapter of this Book. Connecting Prospect's dreams to the business opportunity is critical!

(4) SUMMARY OF COMPENSATION OR PAY PLAN

Once again appropriate brevity is important in introducing Prospects to a potentially complicated subject such as the Pay Plan. Just enough to cover the basics but not overwhelming in technicality or over-hyped in terms of astronomical earnings that would strain the credibility of the business opportunity.

(5) CONCLUSION WITH QUESTIONS AND FINAL RECOGNITIONS

After a fast-paced hour or *less*, a definitive conclusion is an appropriate call for action, and responses to objections that might not have been raised or answered in satisfactory detail earlier in the Presentation. Lastly if appropriate, final Recognitions can be made especially to highlight new Representatives whose Guests may be inspired to sign up and join the Company.

WHAT MAKES A GREAT PRESENTATION?

A great Presentation has to gain and hold the attention of Guests and Prospects. The Presenter should be able to move and inspire, especially with personal stories and a genuine style. If the Presentation is customized to the specific audience members, there will be appeal to both emotions and intellect for a positive decision by Prospects to either join the Company outright or be opened up to the possibilities of the great concept of Network Marketing that are embodied by the MLM Company's products and business opportunity.

21 Ps™

WORLD'S SUREST...FASTEST...SYSTEM FOR MONEY & SUCCESS...MLM CUSTOM GUIDEBOOK

PRESENTATION OF COMPANY BENEFITS (NOT JUST FEATURES)

In Presentations (and Appointments) the vast difference between Features and Benefits in the mind of the Prospect must be realized. Every feature mentioned or discussed must be presented as a benefit for the Prospect whose prime concern is "what can all these products or any 'opportunity' do for me".

BENEFITS OF NETWORK MARKETING IN GENERAL AS EXEMPLIFIED BY THE MLM COMPANY

The days of being defensive about Network Marketing are past. MLM is a proven concept that has captivated the interest of the mainstream economy from investors, market analysts and non-MLM companies that have been outperformed and out-competed by their direct selling counterparts. In good *and* bad economic conditions, MLM companies both new and established have grown in profits, market share and Representatives globally! The benefit for Prospects even with good jobs is the income leverage of MLM that breaks the model of trading personal hours for a salary rate. For those business-owners who are in reality "owned" by their businesses, the benefits are the MLM advantages of business freedom and flexibility. For those who are looking for a business or unemployed or underemployed, the value of starting an opportunity with a nominal investment make MLM a powerful possibility!

PERSONAL BENEFITS

The MLM Company features (especially the Pay Plan) can be directly presented as benefits when the Prospect's circumstances are considered. The option for flexible and part-time hours as well as working from home is attractive to the overworked with long exhausting commutes. The benefits of an MLM business that allow for family time and travel go to the heart of Prospect wants and desires. The ability to set one's own schedule and not be managed or "bossed around" are benefits that are enticing though scary. The Prospect can of course be reassured that the full Team of Sponsor, upline and the entire Company are all there for guidance and support. The Prospect will have a new empowering "family" with a Sponsor who will be a caring mentor with a direct stake in the Prospect's success!

SPECIFIC COMPANY AND PAY PLAN BENEFITS

The benefits of the Pay Plan can be further emphasized with the mighty concept of Leverage. When someone can earn from personal efforts magnified by the production of his or her Team, the income numbers are impressive. The exponential and "generational" features of the MLM Pay Plan are irresistible attractions and tie in to what the Prospect envisions for herself and her family and loved ones!

Even the MLM corporate features of the business opportunity can be expressed as Prospect benefits. Perhaps totally different from other corporate business models, the MLM Company *works for* the Representative. Accounting, website creation, marketing, finance and distribution are essential functions provided by the MLM Corporate Headquarters. Even the polished corporate image (complete with logos, advertising, promotions and the probable legendary Founder or respected Leader) is an asset that the Representative can use to the full. Remember that the Prospect-turned-Representative will have chosen the MLM Company and not the other way around, as in "normal" Companies looking for employees.

PRODUCT OR SERVICE BENEFITS

Even with the MLM Company's main Products or Services, features must be presented as benefits. How do these Products or Services actually help, improve or enhance the lives of Customers? In the end *all* features of the products or services must appeal to the desires of the Prospect and be substantiated by facts.

21 Ps™

WORLD'S SUREST...FASTEST...SYSTEM FOR MONEY & SUCCESS...MLM CUSTOM GUIDEBOOK

CHAPTER 12
PRESENTATIONS, APPOINTMENTS & MORE REFINEMENTS OF MLM SYSTEM

THE IDEAL APPOINTMENTS (ONE-TO-ONE/TWO OR TWO TO ONE/TWO)

The Appointment that is between a Representative and an MLM Prospect (either an individual or a couple) or between a Sponsor accompanied by a new Representative and Prospect(s) is akin to a mini Presentation whose elements were just discussed. The personal Appointment will have its own dynamics with the similar objectives of engaging the Prospect by discovering their wants, circumstances and problems so that benefits can be presented and thus can be determined if the products or the business opportunity is right for the Prospect (*and* also importantly if the Prospect is right for the business!).

CONSULTATIVE "SELLING"

LISTENING

Appointments are usually filled with some anxiety that is felt by both Prospect and new MLM Representative. The Prospect may be apprehensive of being "tried to be sold something" while the Representative has tension and worries about being rejected. If instead, the Representative has the genuine intention to really listen and not even worry about a sale then the Appointment can be actually pleasant and ironically be truly fruitful (in that a sale is naturally made and the Prospect will become truly committed to the products or opportunity)!

ASKING

Asking questions of discovery and problem-solving comes after genuine listening. These are questions to probe what the Prospect really wants, not as questions that are meant to get answers to jump right in and immediately offer the product or business opportunity. Asking is a process of interaction to reveal to the Representative *and* the Prospect *himself or herself* true motivations, needs and desires that may or *may not* be connected to the products or the opportunity.

CONFIRMING

If after confirmation and a true meeting of minds and hearts is achieved because the product or opportunity can in fact fulfill the *current* needs, circumstances and desires of the Prospect then the product or opportunity can be presented as a *possible* solution for the Prospect. This is the stage that verifies that the sincere listening and the candid asking and answering have produced an accurate understanding of where the Prospect is coming from.

PROBLEM-SOLVING AND MOVING FORWARD OR MOVING ON

If there is in fact an honest fit between product or service, or the MLM business opportunity, then the Prospect can on their own legitimately decide to buy and use the product or service or enthusiastically join the company. Or the Prospect and the Representative can move on and preserve their relationship.

Even if takes many more Appointments and Presentations to find this type of Prospect to become a team-member, the organization will enjoy incredible success because the Prospect will become the best kind of Representative: committed and dedicated to the products or services and the motivated development of the MLM business opportunity. Representatives (seasoned and new) will find themselves being less apprehensive and more determined to do even more "Prospecting" that naturally lead to more Appointments and Presentations that result in ultimate success!

21 Ps™

WORLD'S SUREST...FASTEST...SYSTEM FOR MONEY & SUCCESS...MLM CUSTOM GUIDEBOOK

MORE REFINEMENTS OF PRESENTATIONS AND APPOINTMENTS

THE ART and SCIENCE OF GETTING BETTER

GENERAL COMMUNICATIONS, LANGUAGE and STYLES

Presentations, Appointments and many interactions in Network Marketing require some proficiency if not mastery of communications. Even if there are many styles of communication, they all center on language and rapport.

Communications are important not just for the presenter or provider of knowledge and advice but also the receiver of the information. Communication is after all an exchange and an interaction. For example in Presentations and Appointments it is just as important for the Prospect to be detailed and accurate in answers and messages as it is for the MLM Representative to have precise and appropriate points and questions. To discover true needs and wants requires that communication be clear and understandable between parties.

Of course, words make up only a small portion (some experts say only 7%) of communications, while body language, gestures, facial expressions and tone of voice make up the rest. The exchanges of information that establish rapport and the ability to share commonality and mutual understanding if not agreement require that the audience of one or many and the presenter or communicator be "on the same page". It is rapport that paves the way to bonding, respect and potential mutual benefits shared in a successful MLM business.

A word about public speaking which is a dread or mental obstacle for most people, especially those who feel they are not naturally extroverted or articulate or even experienced in business. First of all, even the most "inarticulate" or shy or insecure people can still speak with effectiveness in front of any audience. The keys are just a little courage to try and the mentality that they have to be no more than to be themselves. Remember their best audience is probably people like them, people who can readily identify with common backgrounds and universal needs and desires. Any person can speak from the heart, imparting their own story that can move others, especially if the speaker is new to the business and someone with the admirable motivation to seek success for himself and others!

REPETITION, PRACTICE and the FUNDAMENTALS

To improve one's communication skills in Network Marketing requires actually doing presentations, appointments and public speaking regardless of current competence. Through repetition and practice and more repetition and practice, the new Representative will find their own style that can convey knowledge, information and solutions. Just like any human endeavor that demands excellence to join the ranks of the successful such as sports, music, academics and the arts, the practice and constant application of the fundamentals lead to competence and a person's own unique mastery. One can model and learn from the great MLM practitioners to gain expertise and become better and better.

On a practical note regarding Presentations that often involve 2 or 3 or more Presenters, it is important to switch roles in the presenting areas of "Introduction", "Company/Product Summary", "Compensation Plan", etc. to not only keep the Presentation fresh for the audience (which often includes repeat guests), but also to refine the communications skills of the Presenters themselves.

21 Ps™

WORLD'S SUREST...FASTEST...SYSTEM FOR MONEY & SUCCESS...MLM CUSTOM GUIDEBOOK

CHAPTER 12
PRESENTATIONS, APPOINTMENTS & MORE REFINEMENTS OF MLM SYSTEM

PROGRAM EXERCISE 1
LIST & DESCRIBE SPECIFIC BENEFITS FOR THE PROSPECT OF YOUR PRODUCTS/OPPORTUNITY:

_____

_____

_____

_____

_____

_____

_____

_____

PROGRAM EXERCISE 2
RATE YOUR CURRENT COMMUNICATION SKILLS
(IN PRESENTATIONS OR APPOINTMENTS OR PUBLIC SPEAKING):
Describe your style: Are you a "story-teller" type? An "audio-visual type"? A "read from notes" type? An "ad-libber" or "impromptu/informal" type? Remember to use the type you are comfortable with, but just get better. Model others of your similar type or put in a few elements from other good or great communicators.

_____

_____

_____

_____

_____

_____

_____

_____

21 Ps™

WORLD'S SUREST...FASTEST...SYSTEM FOR MONEY & SUCCESS...MLM CUSTOM GUIDEBOOK

CHAPTER 13
PROCESS: SIGN-UPS (BEFORE/AFTER), TEAM-BUILDING & CREATING LEADERS

Process can be defined as "a series of actions or steps systematically taken over time in order to achieve a particular end." Network Marketing can really be conceived of as the Networking of Process: the actions and steps of a System that ideally lead to money and true success. Or as formulated in Chapter 5 on "Patterning and Duplication" in this Book's System of "21 Ps": <u>Leading and motivating an ever enlarging group of impassioned people to perform the same steps and actions consistently and continuously toward success!</u>

The Introduction of the MLM concept with its opportunity and accompanying products or services is a Process of exposures, marketing and education. The general public, targeted customers and prospects, and even MLM Representatives themselves all experience the Process of what Network Marketing is supposed to represent and offer. As discussed in detail in Chapter 11, Prospecting of potential MLM partners is also a Process of actions and steps done and redone to offer possible solutions and opportunities to those who might benefit.

Presentations and Appointments also implement the steps and actions of Process. The attitudes and skills applied in presenting the MLM products or services and opportunity all point to the goal of finding the optimal kinds of Prospects who will commit to achievement by implementing the MLM Process themselves. When the new Representative is committed to and has full confidence in the MLM System then he or she can be fully developed and trained to contribute to the success of the MLM team. Expediently team success goes hand-in-hand with individual Representative success.

Process has intrinsic elements that have to be understood and accepted. Process takes *time*, actions and perseverance (covered in detail in Chapter 3). The MLM practitioner must be patient, persistent and committed. He or she must perform seemingly menial tasks (so-called "dirty work") that might be mundane, repetitious and boring. To help overcome the apprehension and often perceived grind of repetition and duplication, this Chapter also covers the principles of "enjoying the moment", "awareness" and "acceptance of the present" in the section "The Power of the Now and Today in MLM".

The power of time will eventually make Process work for the MLM Representative and the MLM Team. Continuous and consistent practice of the steps and actions necessary for meeting stated goals will make time eventually an ally to those who are systematic and persevering. At first small victories will confirm the power of the system until more success will breed more success. Process will make attainment of goals self-fulfilling as everyone becomes more adept and confident of the value of following the system.

To quickly summarize, the MLM Process or System generally are the following Steps/Actions:

1.   Introducing the MLM concept and exposing the MLM opportunity with its products or services
2.   Prospecting for the right individuals (often MLM products' customers) who fit the MLM opportunity
3.   Performing Presentations and making Appointments to get Prospects and Customers or educate them
4.   Sign-up new Representatives and get them started quickly forward to success and duplication
5.   Continuously and consistently develop Representatives, build Team and train (everyone) for Leadership

To make the MLM Success Process take on a reality that can be built upon, one of the most critical steps in the retention of new Representatives and making new Recruits become contributing Team members is to ensure that those newly signed-up start fast and experience the first instances of success.

21 Ps™

WORLD'S SUREST...FASTEST...SYSTEM FOR MONEY & SUCCESS...MLM CUSTOM GUIDEBOOK

CHAPTER 13
PROCESS: SIGN-UPS (BEFORE/AFTER), TEAM-BUILDING & CREATING LEADERS

THE NEW SIGN-UP

The Process is working! After introductions, exposures, follow-ups, presentations, appointments and more following up and perhaps another Presentation (or two) and another Appointment (or two) a Prospect has decided to join the MLM Company. Signing up (sponsoring) a new MLM recruit is a satisfying triumph!

Now the greatest MLM challenges in the quest for money and success start for both the new Representative and Sponsor. The steps and actions that led to the sign-up are of course the system of duplication that the new Representative has been shown and must now also follow. Upon signing up, the next 48 hours are critical. The next week or two will set the foundation for the new Team member. The next 30 days to 60 days will determine whether the novice MLM practitioner will be propelled toward earnings, achievements and ultimate success or as some statistics have revealed, the new Representative will join the approximately 80% to 90% who will quit the MLM business within 90 days of starting.

The "Fast-Start" Kit is supposed to jump start the new Representative. It will still be a monumental feat of the new practitioner (with the help or perhaps the hindrance by the Sponsor) to join the ranks who not only stay in the MLM business but reach ultimate and sustained success. The Fast Start Program must indeed be exploited with the support of the Sponsor *and* the MLM team and entire MLM Company.

The Fast Start Kit often includes purchased products and samples, and marketing tools and materials such as brochures, business cards, etc. The Representative's own website (created and linked to the Company) is a powerful component of the modern MLM Practitioner's business arsenal that includes the ability to sign up the new Representative's own Recruits and likely the ability to sell products and services online.

A "fast start" is also the Process of the Sponsor conscientiously and even obsessively supporting and guiding the new Representative in the immediate, continuous and consistent practice and application of the MLM Company's and the MLM Team's duplicable steps and actions to success: the *System*. Especially the process and system of finding new Customers and Prospects that will encourage and excite the new Representative. The diligent Sponsor who thoroughly supports his or her own new downline is exhibiting the behaviors that the new Representative will enact when he or she also becomes a Sponsor.

The new MLM Representative must also be taught to maximize his or her outlook for survival and success by engaging in the MLM opportunity as his or her *real* business, no matter if engaged in full-time or part-time (which is what most new Representatives will only have the time or inclination for). In consultation with the Representative's legal and financial advisors (ideally a business Attorney and CPA), the following business basics must be addressed:

1. Business Entity (most will start as a sole proprietorship, even as husband and wife)
2. Basic Accounting System (computerized) for tax purposes in addition to the MLM Company's
3. Structuring the Business Environment at Home: for both organizational and tax reasons
4. Overall organization of the business including materials, tools, products and schedules
5. Miscellaneous such as insurance, investing in personal marketing and considering partners, etc.

A highly motivated new Representative with a great Sponsor in a good MLM Company can count on support.

21 Ps™

WORLD'S SUREST...FASTEST...SYSTEM FOR MONEY & SUCCESS...MLM CUSTOM GUIDEBOOK

CHAPTER 13
PROCESS: SIGN-UPS (BEFORE/AFTER), TEAM-BUILDING & CREATING LEADERS

TEAM BUILDING

The new Representative upon signing up has joined a Team: a dynamic group that must grow in numbers and effectiveness as an organization in order for the individual to prosper. The new Representative, because of the nature of Network Marketing actually belongs to an overlap of Teams, his Sponsor's and Upline's Team that he or she has joined, the MLM Company as the overarching team, and his or her own potential Team that can be started and developed as the new Representative's downline.

The Team is in fact the context where Process and System are demonstrated, practiced and improved as each team member (Representative) performs the Steps and Actions according to his or her own skills that produce the requisite results. While each individual Representative as a team member will largely determine his or her own level of success, whatever results he or she can produce can be amplified and supported by other MLM Team members that for example can model achievement or can function in routine ways such as being the Presenters at Meetings or Mentors or Legitimizers of the MLM concept.

The best Teams are products of the best-applied systems. There can be many somewhat different systems as long as they abide by the basics of the MLM Processes of Introduction and Exposures; Prospecting; Presenting and Appointments; Representative Sign-Ups and Start-Ups; and ultimately the development of Individual and Team Leadership. When individuals are empowered by support and challenge, they respond! People will often do more for others or because of the influence of others than on their own. In turn the motivated can motivate others to do the same or better in the spirit of friendly competition or newly-ignited ambitions.

Teams are of course natural occurrences in human affairs, from the team of family, neighborhood or community, workplace in corporations or small business, or even nations. The MLM teams of Sponsor/Representative lines are unique in that typically an individual is directly rewarded and compensated by the success of a created team of individuals (the downline) who are developed to even ideally surpass the Leader. Support for others leverages one's own success!

The MLM Team empowers individuals because the common purpose and objectives of the group benefit individuals. The process and the system harness the efforts of the many for access to any individual who wishes to "plug in" and get support. The MLM Company recognizes and promotes the power of Team through its Pay and Compensation Plans as well as the human elements of recognition and status rewards. Not only is there a sense of belonging in an MLM Team, there is a sense of excitement with concrete prizes and bonuses.

Another exciting aspect of Team building in MLM is the notion of open entry. There are no mandated barriers or requirements or policies or set standards other than the need to work hard and smart and to follow a proven process and system that has worked for others and will work for any ordinary individual who desires to be extraordinary!

The ultimate manifestation of a Team' excellence is Leadership that brings results. Once again, MLM is unique in that Leadership is democratic and fluid and unexpectedly can be sustainable without having to wrest power from anyone. Everyone can in fact be a Leader in an MLM team. In fact the more Leaders the better as organizations and teams can be expanded and diversified. The phenomenon of Leadership is further covered later in this Chapter and in Chapter 14 on "Promotions, Meetings and Trainings".

<u>21 Ps</u>™

WORLD'S SUREST...FASTEST...SYSTEM FOR MONEY & SUCCESS...MLM CUSTOM GUIDEBOOK

CHAPTER 13
PROCESS: SIGN-UPS (BEFORE/AFTER), TEAM-BUILDING & CREATING LEADERS

THE POWER of the NOW and TODAY in MLM

PROCESS, AWARENESS AND LEARNING

Process requires being in the moment because there is no other reality. When you are in the MLM system at whatever stage and if the system is genuinely adhered to with the expectation of success, the only question is will you perform the step or action? What is important *now*? What am I learning *now*? How can I make the most out of this moment? The past is irreversible and the future is only imaginable.

The sense of awareness of a particular action or step, be it consulting with Prospects, or learning about products or services, or being trained and guided by Mentors, or doing follow-ups or marketing serves to maximize the effectiveness of the moment and to minimize the tension or anxiety of any doubts or fears.

ENJOYING THE MOMENT

As you build on small successes and accomplishments, your sense of belief increases and what was once dreaded can be possibly considered fun. Those who make whatever work they have as play are more effective and happier. But then again, what else is necessary to make you "happy"?

At this very moment, you are alive and anything is possible. You have all you need in health, ability, intelligence, resources and support. What difference does it make if you fret about the moment or not? Actually any doubt or fear will not be as fruitful as expecting the good and the positive. What you project you generally attract in the particular moment. Enjoy the moment because it will never be here again!

ACCEPTANCE OF THE PRESENT

What actually sabotages the moment is the lack of acceptance of what is and being worried about the outcome of the particular step or action. If you have learned and practiced and have seen the results of what the step or action may bring, then what is the point of not being fully engaged in the moment?

Perhaps deep in the recesses of your mind lie the past stories of "failures" or "disappointments". They are just stories that you have interpreted and accepted as "truths" and "beliefs" that may be unconnected to what were real and true. Your ego relishes judgments and engages in "story telling" to explain "reality".

However the moment of performing the action or step of a process is neutral. Whatever result is subject to interpretation. There will be new results and outcomes, and now you can be convinced of actual facts and evidence. So if you actually detach yourself from the outcome (not worry about what happens) then you can actually make the outcome better or at least become less stressed and also become a better performer.

These present moments of today's steps and actions taken in whatever circumstances will be remembered as "the good old times", when everything was still possible, when you were young (certainly "younger" if the remembrance is 10 or 20 years in the distance), when you were first excited to the breakthroughs of your potential, when you were fully alive and able to meet any hardship or challenge, and when you started and continued on the lifelong journey of new ventures and adventures that were once still uncertain but you have now made into wondrous outcomes!

21 Ps™

WORLD'S SUREST...FASTEST...SYSTEM FOR MONEY & SUCCESS...MLM CUSTOM GUIDEBOOK

CREATING NEW MLM LEADERS

With the outlook of emphasizing the critical nature of Process and duplicating a System, *new* Leaders must be created. These recently empowered MLM Representatives must possess and display certain attributes that can be modeled, traits and qualities that propel them to further and greater Leadership. Team growth only occurs with the proliferation of Leaders. Unique to MLM, there can be many "chiefs" in an ongoing drive to share the power, responsibility and rewards of leading and motivating people. A Leader who creates more Leaders like him or her does not relinquish power but actually gains organizationally and monetarily!

SOME OF THE PRIMARY TRAITS AND QUALITIES OF *NEW* MLM LEADERS:

1. Are Coachable and Trainable:
New Leaders learn process and system, apply actions/steps and are able to coach and train others.

2. Know their Life Purpose:
New Leaders know what is most important to them and why; they discover what really drives them.

3. Produce:
New Leaders participate in the *virtuous* cycle. They produce good results that lead to even better results.

4. Persevere:
New Leaders have become Leaders because they meet challenges, make any necessary changes and don't quit.

5. Project their Personal Power:
New Leaders learn the skills of excellence, practice self-discipline and believe in the power of teamwork.

6. Practice the MLM Company's culture and mission:
Doing due-diligence to find the right Company's, new Leaders apply the best principles and purposes.

7. Are deeply knowledgeable about the MLM Company's Products or Services:
New Leaders eagerly learn everything about their products so they can teach and educate others.

8. Lead by example:
Using the Company's products or services makes Leaders know benefits; Credibility is genuine.

9. Are "Self-Improvers":
Even as new Leaders are comfortable with being themselves, they strive to get better in every way.

10. Are mentally tough and physically fit:
New Leaders have the inner and external wherewithal to confront trials and seize opportunities.

21 Ps™

WORLD'S SUREST...FASTEST...SYSTEM FOR MONEY & SUCCESS...MLM CUSTOM GUIDEBOOK

CHAPTER 13
PROCESS: SIGN-UPS (BEFORE/AFTER), TEAM-BUILDING & CREATING LEADERS

CHAPTER EXERCISE 1
WHAT IS YOUR MLM TEAM'S PROCESS and SYSTEM?
List and briefly describe the actual Steps and Actions:

_____

_____

_____

_____

_____

CHAPTER EXERCISE 2
RATE YOUR MLM TEAM'S PROCESS and SYSTEM:

_____

_____

_____

CHAPTER EXERCISE 3
WHAT IS YOUR MLM COMPANY'S "FAST START" PROGRAM?
What are the actual Tools, Materials or Procedures?

_____

_____

_____

CHAPTER EXERCISE 4
RATE YOUR MLM COMPANY'S "FAST START" PROGRAM:

_____

_____

_____

21 Ps™

WORLD'S SUREST...FASTEST...SYSTEM FOR MONEY & SUCCESS...MLM CUSTOM GUIDEBOOK

CHAPTER 14
PROMOTIONS, MARKETING and TRAINING SESSIONS FOR LEADERS (EVERYONE!)

Promotions in the context of the MLM Team are defined in three main ways in this Chapter. First is the model of Rank Promotions as in the various levels of Representative positions starting with the status of the new Sign-up (called Representative or Distributor or Associate, etc.) and progressing to some level of "management" (sponsorship) with titles such as Director or Manager and then advancing to often "wider" management with the higher ranks of Regional Director or Regional Manager.

Promotional Ranks are generally achieved by the number of direct Recruits and overall group volume of sales of the entire downline, with a minimal level of personal sales required to maintain the achieved rank and the ability to receive commissions on group sales. The uppermost Ranks are reached when a Leader has built a large, wide and deep organization. Recruits may number in the thousands and total sales volumes of the group may be in the millions. These "superstars" are called National Managers or Directors or perhaps something glamorous as "Diamond" or "Five Star" or "Platinum" Directors.

The second meaning of Promotions in this Chapter has to do with team building and the idea of creative techniques to draw Customers and Prospects to grow the organization to produce sales volumes and new Representatives. Various tactics and methods will be explored briefly that are also described in Special Tools 4 ("Creative Marketing", page 158) that belong in such categories as Advertising, Business Promotions, Public Events, Private Parties and High-Tech Marketing.

The creativity of business marketing techniques to capture Customers for products and Prospects for the MLM business opportunity allows for the varying personalities and abilities of the MLM team members to use tactics and methods that are a fit. The ideal promotional methods should be cost-effective or essentially free except for the application of effort, time and ingenuity. There are infinite ways to attract people who will buy and consider the MLM opportunity if people see genuine benefits and solutions that are promoted by honest, competent and caring network-marketers.

When Promotions result in the building and growth of the MLM Team, the critical need for proper and powerful Training surfaces. The enlarging organization has the opportunity to make itself great and self-sustaining. The organization's system must be practiced and refined and duplicated. The process must allow those who will offer their dedication, work ethic and commitment to self-improvement to be matched by the team's support systems to teach, train and amplify efforts in a continuous advance to higher incomes and true success! Effective and continuous Trainings comprise the 3rd meaning of Promotions in this Chapter.

The structure and contents of formal Trainings must be created in ways that actually produce concrete and positive outcomes. Teaching must generate real improvement that can be practically applied. If someone is taught to prospect and market, there must be tangible success that confirms the effectiveness of the instruction. Coaching must be personalized to take into account individual strengths and weaknesses so that for example if someone is coached to become a better public speaker, the trainee must learn to be an enhanced communicator of concepts and information in their own unique style that has been improved.

Trainings must actually yield fast and lasting results so that the trainee gains competence, confidence and belief. Trainings can only be considered successful if there are measurable positive outcomes such as more motivated Prospects or more (very) satisfied Customers. This Chapter will present actual Training Topics and concrete Training Sessions such as the results-promised "SUDU" (Super Duplication) 30-Day Drives which can be considered Super Trainings (and Super Promotions!) of the "21Ps" of this Book.

21 Ps™

WORLD'S SUREST...FASTEST...SYSTEM FOR MONEY & SUCCESS...MLM CUSTOM GUIDEBOOK

CHAPTER 14
PROMOTIONS, MARKETING and TRAINING SESSIONS FOR LEADERS (EVERYONE!)

THE STRUCTURE OF TRAINING SESSIONS
The overall structure and multiple elements of an intense Training session will be illustrated in a "SUDU" (Super Duplication) 30-Day Drive described later in this Chapter. The following also applies to Trainings or Coaching in general:

SCHEDULE
Trainings should be regular and continuous. As soon as someone signs up for the business opportunity, Trainings should be scheduled. Each member of the MLM Team must commit to their particular Training schedule and abide by it. The level of time and effort commitment will equal the explicit income and recruitment objectives of each Representative.

LOCATION
Trainings can be conducted at an office, a place of business, a hotel meeting or conference room, or at a home. Size appropriate to the number of participants, convenience, costs, and availability are factors in considering location. In the "SUDU" (Super Duplication) 30-Day Drive, Trainings are conducted in all available locations but ideally headquartered in a home for maximum convenience, cost savings and as will be shown later, intensity, excitement and effectiveness.

TOPICS AND TOOLS
A Training session can focus on a specific topic such as "Prospecting-Partnering", "Dream-Building", "Appointments" or "Product Knowledge" or can be a comprehensive or part of a series of related topics that are always necessary to gain and maintain both fundamental knowledge and new expertise/skills. The tools will be appropriate to the topic and level of knowhow of participants and can include Manuals, DVDs, Web Trainings, Books, Tapes, etc.

TYPES AND METHODS OF TRAINING
While Trainings can be conducted one-to-one and even on the phone, the most impactful are Trainings that involve a unified Team or group that is motivated or made to be motivated to succeed. Low cost or free venues such as YouTube, Skype and commercial web-based conferencing are powerful ways to reach many Team members conveniently and engagingly. Still nothing beats the face-to-face interactions of excited Representatives with clear objectives and goals for unequivocal results!

PARTICIPANTS and INTENSITY
Trainees must be treated as Leaders-in-the-Making. The new or seasoned Representative will respond to and be energized by a concrete outcome such as a new Customer or a Prospect who signs up as a direct or even immediate consequence of Training. Team members working together, encouraging, supporting and challenging each other amplify the achievement of single individuals. Even such powerful techniques as Role-Playing and Team Brainstorming can best be deployed by Teams. A group of excited, driven and powerfully led Representatives can accomplish incredible results as will be illustrated by the dynamics and electricity of intense Training Sessions such as a "SUDU" (Super Duplication) 30-Day Drive.

TRAINER(S)
The Group of Trainers should include the Sponsor, successful Representatives in the downline with various abilities and experience, and even special outside Trainers expert in development, motivation, leadership and other specialized areas. The "21 Ps" as a System can be used by Sponsors and Team Leaders. Intense and powerful Trainings such as a SUDU 30-Day Drive will optimally be conducted by a special Training Consultant or an absolutely committed (obsessed-for-success) Sponsor.

CHAPTER 14
PROMOTIONS, MARKETING and TRAINING SESSIONS FOR LEADERS (EVERYONE!)

CREATIVE MARKETING

Many new MLM Representatives for several of their own personal or perceived reasons are hesitant to approach their "Warm Market" (the group of people who knows him or her well such as family, good friends or close associates). Furthermore the "warm" circle of influence is inherently limited in number even if family and friends would be good starting points to MLM marketing. Perhaps, this familiar group can be considered later. Thus with the perspective that everyone who can benefit from the MLM products or the business opportunity are prospects, it becomes a matter of creativity and imagination to find the basically infinite number of candidates to the MLM offerings. Below are a few of the countless sources and methods of MLM growth in sales and Recruits.

ADVERTISING

Even if MLM is supposed to be fundamentally "word-of-mouth", advertising (especially low cost or "free") can result in sales and leads. Depending on budgets and the analyzed or proven rates of success, the MLM Team, Sponsor or individual Representative can consider classified advertising in newspapers, other print media or consumer websites such as Craigslist, etc. Direct mail campaigns or distributing neighborhood flyers are also strategies to employ as well as cooperative advertising-marketing with non-competing businesses.

BUSINESS PROMOTIONS

Acknowledging that the MLM opportunity is indeed a business, all Representatives must be walking (or "driving") promotions themselves. At all appropriate times, each MLM Practitioner must carry business cards, opportunity and product brochures or catalogs, as well as all necessary tools that are available from the Company and the organization. The handed-out CD or DVD or Audio Tape or Article Reprint or MLM book might just end up in the possession of the Prospect who becomes the next star downline-Representative. Even cars or trucks of MLM practitioners should be actual vehicles of promotion that have at least a bumper sticker or two if not outright car signs (for the boldly inspired Representative!)

PUBLIC EVENTS and PRIVATE PARTIES

Public events can be formal and informal venues for the MLM product and opportunity. Those with the ideal MLM products that can take advantage of demonstrations and visual displays can be shown at trade shows, fairs, festivals and flea markets upon consideration of the costs, viability and the returns of investment in time and money. At the other end of the spectrum, a "private" party is another setting to interact with people. In fact some MLM Companies such as Pampered Chef, Tupperware, PartyLite and Discovery Toys explicitly use the Party Plan as its main way to present products and opportunities.

HIGH-TECH MARKETING

In addition to the convenience and powerful resources of the Representative's individual websites for business and customer/organizational management (that most MLM Companies routinely and expertly provide each Representative), there is the amazing capability of internet social networking for connecting the MLM practitioner with his or her spheres of influence that can expand easily and quickly.

The keys to the pervasive, popular and influential web phenomena that are Facebook, LinkedIn and Twitter are the offering of value and the establishment of community. When "Followers" or "Friends" or "Connections" identify for themselves the standbys of benefits and value ("what's in it for me?"), then familiarity, credibility and trust lead to mutually beneficial relationships and sales!

21 Ps™

WORLD'S SUREST...FASTEST...SYSTEM FOR MONEY & SUCCESS...MLM CUSTOM GUIDEBOOK

CHAPTER 14
PROMOTIONS, MARKETING and TRAINING SESSIONS FOR LEADERS (EVERYONE!)

TRAINING TOPIC 1
APPOINTMENTS and PERSONAL PRESENTATIONS

The face-to-face appointment with a Prospect who has agreed to meet an MLM Representative and many times the upline Sponsor is a critical episode. The new Representative or the still unsuccessful Network Marketer must be thoroughly skilled to make the most of the Appointment for his or her business *and* for the sake of the Prospect. The training to gain competence and success in Appointments and Personal Presentations must be centered on "consultative selling" as discussed earlier in Chapter 12.

The best way to conduct this training for Appointments is one-to-one or if in a large group setting, using role-play and simulations between two "players" or among three "actors". The processes of Listening, Asking, Confirming and Problem-Solving must be practiced repeatedly to refine skills and ingrain the attitudes of what may also be called "value selling" and "personal consulting". The objective of the Appointment is to carefully pay attention to the Prospect's words, gestures and overall behavior to discover what he or she truly wants and whether the product(s) or the opportunity meets those wants.

While scripts and wordings of questions and probing inquiries are useful in mastering, what is even more important is for the Network Marketer to genuinely become a Problem-Solver by showing caring and integrity in ascertaining the Prospect's circumstances. Prospects will have many needs and motivations; the MLM Representative must sincerely find the solutions that are ideally embodied in the MLM Company's products or services and business opportunity.

TRAINING TOPIC 2
PROSPECTING TECHNIQUES

This Training can include *actual* Prospecting in *real time*! Each Trainee's own Special Lists of Prospects can be developed with various Exercises. Whether the Lists are created from "Warm Markets" or "Referrals" or "Creative Marketing", Prospects can be contacted *during* the Training! A good way is to engage in "Instant Messaging" or "Tweeting" that notifies Prospects of your current MLM Training. The "post", message or "tweet" must be appealing not as a sales pitch but as something of social value, something considered at least interesting if not immediately actable as an overall proposition to buy a product or join an opportunity. "Followers", "Connections" or "Friends" can be drawn to a process of information, current happenings and MLM activities that can eventually produce Customers and Prospects.

TRAINING TOPIC 3
MLM Product or Service Demonstration

A Training in Products or Services can also yield concrete results if the training material can be made "live" and the trainees made animated in their actual "performance" *during* the training session. This can be accomplished by recording the session, especially on YouTube. If good enough, the live training becomes another tool for future prospecting for and legitimizing of the MLM Company while making the actual session dynamic and lively. "The world is watching!"

The above Training topics and techniques are part of a wide-ranging system of developing Leaders that will make individuals and the Team more expert, effective and successful. Imagine if leader development and MLM results can be intensified, amplified and time-condensed to 30 days! See next!

21 Ps™

WORLD'S SUREST...FASTEST...SYSTEM FOR MONEY & SUCCESS...MLM CUSTOM GUIDEBOOK

THE "SUDU" (SUPER DUPLICATION) 30-DAY DRIVE

The "SUDU (Super Duplication) 30-Day Drive is a special training and business development program that is a comprehensive campaign meant to quickly start or jumpstart the concrete results for individual MLM Representatives and the entire Team or Organization! Expect doubling or tripling of *income* and the number of quality Prospects who will join the business opportunity! Anticipate an overflow of excited Customers and a deluge of superior leads for more Customers and Prospects! These are some elements of the SUDU Drive:

An absolute commitment for a Sponsor and key Representative(s) to apply the Team's MLM System.

Designating for 30 days the use of a (Home) Headquarters or "War Room" to conduct/centralize "operations".

Creating excitement and urgency in a continuous stream of concrete activities such as:
Prospecting
Presentations
Gatherings
Appointments
Parties
Special Meetings
Strategy Sessions
Group Brainstorming
Product or Service Demonstrations
Development Trainings
Sharing of Tools and Techniques
Invitations of "Special Guests"
Recording of sessions on YouTube or other media
Three-way Callings
Massive Remote Conferencing
Product "Sales"
Video Presentations
Role-Playing and Simulations
Neighborhood Specials
Community Events
Team Rallies
Special Missions

The SUDU (Super Duplication) 30-Day Drive will require the concentration of effort and resources with the intention of having fun and generating incredible concrete results! Creativity and passion will be combined with innovative strategies and logistics. There have to be preparation and planning and execution. There have to be accommodation and flexibility to implement or change actions to suit individuals or circumstances. There must be demonstrations and applications of leadership that inspire and set examples.

From the practical standpoint, there must be an overall coordinator of the SUDU 30-Day Drive. This can be a Sponsor or a seasoned (and very motivated) MLM Representative or outside Consultant. Ideally a comprehensive "best-results" system must be utilized such as this Book's "21 Ps" that incorporates an MLM Company's and MLM Team's policies, processes and philosophy. See more "SUDU" details on pages 159-161.

<u>21 Ps</u>™

WORLD'S SUREST...FASTEST...SYSTEM FOR MONEY & SUCCESS...MLM CUSTOM GUIDEBOOK

CHAPTER 14
PROMOTIONS, MARKETING and TRAINING SESSIONS FOR LEADERS (EVERYONE!)

CHAPTER EXERCISE 1
Ask yourself as a new (or motivated) Representative what Training Topic you are interested in to produce the results you are seeking in your MLM business.

_____

_____

_____

_____

_____

As a Sponsor, analyze and consult with a Recruit or direct downline to ascertain his or her specific Training need(s) with the intent and expectation to produce fast and lasting results. (You can do this for any or all of your downline Representatives.)

_____

_____

_____

_____

_____

_____

As a Representative or Sponsor, ask what you are good at or what you can become good or expert at in order to be a Trainer in your preferred area. (Ask this of others in your organization.)

_____

_____

_____

_____

_____

_____

21 Ps™

WORLD'S SUREST...FASTEST...SYSTEM FOR MONEY & SUCCESS...MLM CUSTOM GUIDEBOOK

CHAPTER 15
PINNACLE OF SUCCESS: PUTTING IT ALL TOGETHER + EPILOGUE

There are many excellent books on Success in general and MLM Wealth as a particular subject. There are many superlative tools and programs such as seminars, tapes, CDs and coaching and training sessions. These books and tools have been written and produced by proven trainers and very successful MLM practitioners who have learned, refined and applied the success principles and systems for achievement in the actual arenas of the MLM marketplaces.

These success systems work! But why aren't more successful in MLM? Why do more than 70% of new Representatives quit an MLM Company within 90 days? And within a year perhaps only 10% of the new Representatives are earning any income? Of course not everyone uses the success systems or applies them diligently. In fact the majority of those who even engage in training of some sort have made their efforts at self-improvement and personal development as lackluster and as routinely uninspiring as all their MLM activities.

What is needed is urgency or a new sense of immediacy no matter where one is in the MLM success spectrum. If you find and use a success program, use it every day! Use is intensely and obsessively! For example, use this Book and its "21 Ps" system every single day! Or engage in your own 30-Day SUDU (Super Duplication) Drives with your present team or created team! You can utilize the elements outlined on Page 101 above or formulate a "formal" Consultant-coordinated or Sponsored-led 30-Day Drive or one that *you* start as detailed in Special Tools 4 (Creative Marketing / "SUDU" (Super Duplication) 30-Day Drives).

We all know what we need to do and be in order to succeed. The question is will we do "it"? Or more practically how can we make ourselves do what is necessary or be made to do what is necessary? Discover, learn, believe, execute, correct if needed, continue executing, build and keep building, succeed and enjoy each moment! The *Pinnacle* of Success is scaled every day in every way!

From the practical standpoint, no matter the "success system" employed, the new MLM Representative must start with their own development. In this Book of the "21 Ps" System, SECTION 1 covers Purpose, Productivity, Perseverance, Power and Patterning (Modeling/Duplication).

Mastery of these foundational "5Ps" comes first. Any attempt at the "technical" activities of Prospecting and Presentations or Product Demonstrations are undermined or sabotaged by a Representative who is not driven by a compelling Purpose, or who is inefficient or ineffective personally, or who gives up easily, or is incapable of self-management and empowering communications, or who does not master modeling those who have already succeeded.

If the new Representative has some level of present and continuing self-mastery then the knowledge, skills and proficiencies learned and applied in SECTION 2 and SECTION 3 of this Book of "21 Ps" will be a matter of training and absolute commitment to acquire. When the Representative profoundly realizes that he or she *is* the opportunity, anything is possible and achievement is inevitable!

How amazing it is to discover that what the MLM business is really about is that one is provided with an exceptional vehicle for self-improvement and personal empowerment. It becomes more than selling products or services or prospecting or recruiting business partners. It goes beyond money and status. What really matters is that you become a better person, a person who cares and contributes to the welfare of others, and a person who has made the most of your unique abilities and talents to accomplish your heart's dreams and desires. It just so happens that you also provide the benefits of great Products or Services to your Customers and life-changing Opportunities to partners in business and life!

21 Ps™

WORLD'S SUREST...FASTEST...SYSTEM FOR MONEY & SUCCESS...MLM CUSTOM GUIDEBOOK

CHAPTER 15
PINNACLE OF SUCCESS: PUTTING IT ALL TOGETHER + EPILOGUE

BLANK PAGE FOR

CHAPTER 15

NOTES

21 Ps™

WORLD'S SUREST...FASTEST...SYSTEM FOR MONEY & SUCCESS...MLM CUSTOM GUIDEBOOK

Epilogue: The Final 3 "Ps"

The 15 main "Ps" of Multi-Level/Network Marketing (Purpose, Productivity, Perseverance, Power, Patterning, Proposition, Product, People, Pricing, Pay, Prospecting, Presentations, Process, Promotions and Pinnacle of Success) are taught and applied as Principles, Practices and Programs (the First 3 Ps). The final "3 Ps" are also universal concepts that overlay the MLM Success System: Prosumer-Consumer, Profits and Planet.

"Prosumer" is a term coined by the thinker, author and futurist, Alvin Toffler to describe the modern consumer in the age of high technology and global telecommunications as someone who not only consumes but also produces in the global economy.

Think of ATM s (Automated Teller Machines) and Buffet Restaurants and Self-Pay Grocery Shopping, and Do-it-Yourself Warehouse Stores and Home-Improvement Projects, and now of course on-line banking, electronic shopping and even on-line consumption (and production) of internet social network content that all told would have yearly economic values in the (hundreds of) billions of dollars. In many ways, MLM is a perfect example of "Prosuming" since each MLM Practitioner is both a consumer of the MLM product or service and of course "produces" sales, marketing, distribution, training and personnel (more MLM Recruits).

Profit is of course the overlay of the MLM opportunity and business in general. This "P" underlies the economic activities of MLM and is a factor in business survival, sustainability as well as a general measure of how well individual MLM Participants, Teams and entire Companies are doing.

Profit used to be strictly equated with the "bottom-line". But in modern civilizations and the competing complexities of interests, limitations and conscious choices in global economics, there are many bottom-lines. There are social bottom-lines and there are environmental bottom-lines that Companies, Communities and individuals face in a fragile and finite Planet.

The last "P" (the 21st "P") of Planet is the subject of an entire book or volumes of books. Suffice it to say that humans (consumers, communities, and business people) may have finally realized or at least acknowledge that ALL of daily activities and commercial pursuits and life itself are based on the bounty and protection of Earth systems.

You could have the greatest products or opportunity and make millions or billions of dollars but if the Planet itself degrades to barely habitable environments or some global disaster hits, or if most of the world lives in poverty and injustice, or if there is prevalent hunger and warfare and terrorism, your life wouldn't be worth living if you can in fact stay alive at all.

No economic actions and endeavors are sustainable for profit and existence without the balancing of the final 3 Ps in this Book's system of 21 Ps. Perhaps MLM can contribute to a much better Planet with more People (Prosumers) getting opportunities at Profitable and sustainable livelihoods. Perhaps MLM can even become the dominant economic model that can benefit People-Profits-Planet and our quest to solve our global problems. Only by adhering to the balance and sustenance of People (Prosumers), Profits and Planet can there ever flourish a viable system for even such worldly objectives as "Money and Success"!

21 Ps™
WORLD'S SUREST...FASTEST...SYSTEM FOR MONEY & SUCCESS...MLM CUSTOM GUIDEBOOK

BLANK PAGE

(END OF MAIN BOOK SECTIONS)

21 Ps™
WORLD'S SUREST...FASTEST...SYSTEM FOR MONEY & SUCCESS...MLM CUSTOM GUIDEBOOK

SPECIAL TOOLS 1

TIME-LINES OF GOALS & SUCCESSES:
MONTHLY
TO YEARS 1 to 50

USING THE INFORMATION FROM THE EXERCISES OF CHAPTER 1, "SPECIAL TOOLS" 1 PUTS PURPOSES, MOTIVATIONS AND GOALS ON PAPER.

UNLIKE MOST CALENDARS OR SCHEDULES, THE "21 Ps" SYSTEM STARTS WITH THE "END" FIRST: FROM YEARS "40 - 50" (FROM THE PRESENT) TO "30 - 40" TO "25 – 30" TO "20 – 25" TO "15 – 20" TO "10 – 15" TO "5 – 10" TO "3 – 5" TO "1 – 3" TO "0 – 1" AND THEN TO A TIME LINE OF 6 MONTHS AND THEN FINALLY TO A WEEKLY SCHEDULE THAT GETS DOWN TO DAYS AND HOURS IN THE BONUS CALENDAR STARTING ON PAGE 160!

21 Ps™

WORLD'S SUREST...FASTEST...SYSTEM FOR MONEY & SUCCESS...MLM CUSTOM GUIDEBOOK

SPECIAL TOOLS 1
TIME-LINES OF GOALS & SUCCESSES: WEEKLY/MONTHLY/YEARS 1 TO 50

<u>YEARS 40 TO 50 (FROM CURRENT YEAR)</u>

GOALS:

_____

_____

_____

SUCCESSES:

_____

_____

_____

GOALS FROM PREVIOUS 10 YEARS (YEARS 30 – 40) MET? PROJECT, ENVISION & CONNECT.

_____

SOME DETAILS OF YOUR LIFE IN THESE LAST 10 YEARS (40 – 50 YEARS FORWARD FROM CURRENT):

_____

_____

_____

WARNING:
IF YOU WERE TO DIE THIS 10-YEAR PERIOD, BRIEFLY DECRIBE YOUR "EULOGY" OR BIOGRAPHY,
ESPECIALLY WHAT YOU ACCOMPLISHED AND WHAT LEGACY YOU LEFT BEHIND FOR OTHERS:

_____

_____

_____

21 Ps™

WORLD'S SUREST...FASTEST...SYSTEM FOR MONEY & SUCCESS...MLM CUSTOM GUIDEBOOK

SPECIAL TOOLS 1
TIME-LINES OF GOALS & SUCCESSES: WEEKLY/MONTHLY/YEARS 1 TO 50

YEARS 30 TO 40 (FROM CURRENT YEAR)

GOALS:

_____

_____

_____

SUCCESSES:

_____

_____

_____

GOALS FROM PREVIOUS 5 YEARS (YEARS 25 – 30) MET? PROJECT, ENVISION & CONNECT.

_____

SOME DETAILS OF YOUR LIFE IN THESE LAST 10 YEARS (30 – 40 YEARS FORWARD FROM CURRENT):

_____

_____

_____

WARNING:
IF YOU WERE TO DIE THIS 10-YEAR PERIOD, BRIEFLY DECRIBE YOUR "EULOGY" OR BIOGRAPHY,
ESPECIALLY WHAT YOU ACCOMPLISHED AND WHAT LEGACY YOU LEFT BEHIND FOR OTHERS:

_____

_____

_____

21 Ps™

WORLD'S SUREST...FASTEST...SYSTEM FOR MONEY & SUCCESS...MLM CUSTOM GUIDEBOOK

SPECIAL TOOLS 1
TIME-LINES OF GOALS & SUCCESSES: WEEKLY/MONTHLY/YEARS 1 TO 50

YEARS 25 TO 30 (FROM CURRENT YEAR)

GOALS:

_____

_____

_____

SUCCESSES:

_____

_____

_____

GOALS FROM PREVIOUS 5 YEARS (YEARS 20 – 25) MET? PROJECT, ENVISION & CONNECT.

_____

SOME DETAILS OF YOUR LIFE IN THESE LAST 5 YEARS (25 – 30 YEARS FORWARD FROM CURRENT):

_____

_____

_____

WARNING:
IF YOU WERE TO DIE THIS 5-YEAR PERIOD, BRIEFLY DECRIBE YOUR "EULOGY" OR BIOGRAPHY, ESPECIALLY WHAT YOU ACCOMPLISHED AND WHAT LEGACY YOU LEFT BEHIND FOR OTHERS:

_____

_____

_____

21 Ps™

WORLD'S SUREST...FASTEST...SYSTEM FOR MONEY & SUCCESS...MLM CUSTOM GUIDEBOOK

SPECIAL TOOLS 1
TIME-LINES OF GOALS & SUCCESSES: WEEKLY/MONTHLY/YEARS 1 TO 50

YEARS 20 TO 25 (FROM CURRENT YEAR)

GOALS:

_____

_____

_____

SUCCESSES:

_____

_____

_____

GOALS FROM PREVIOUS 5 YEARS (YEARS 15 – 20) MET? PROJECT, ENVISION & CONNECT.

_____

SOME DETAILS OF YOUR LIFE IN THESE LAST 5 YEARS (20 – 25 YEARS FORWARD FROM CURRENT):

_____

_____

_____

WARNING:
IF YOU WERE TO DIE THIS 5-YEAR PERIOD, BRIEFLY DECRIBE YOUR "EULOGY" OR BIOGRAPHY,
ESPECIALLY WHAT YOU ACCOMPLISHED AND WHAT LEGACY YOU LEFT BEHIND FOR OTHERS:

_____

_____

_____

21 Ps™

WORLD'S SUREST...FASTEST...SYSTEM FOR MONEY & SUCCESS...MLM CUSTOM GUIDEBOOK

SPECIAL TOOLS 1
TIME-LINES OF GOALS & SUCCESSES: WEEKLY/MONTHLY/YEARS 1 TO 50

YEARS 15 TO 20 (FROM CURRENT YEAR)

GOALS:

_____

_____

_____

SUCCESSES:

_____

_____

_____

GOALS FROM PREVIOUS 5 YEARS (YEARS 10 – 15) MET? PROJECT, ENVISION & CONNECT.

_____

SOME DETAILS OF YOUR LIFE IN THESE LAST 5 YEARS (15 – 20 YEARS FORWARD FROM CURRENT):

_____

_____

_____

WARNING:
IF YOU WERE TO DIE THIS 5-YEAR PERIOD, BRIEFLY DECRIBE YOUR "EULOGY" OR BIOGRAPHY, ESPECIALLY WHAT YOU ACCOMPLISHED AND WHAT LEGACY YOU LEFT BEHIND FOR OTHERS:

_____

_____

_____

21 Ps™

WORLD'S SUREST...FASTEST...SYSTEM FOR MONEY & SUCCESS...MLM CUSTOM GUIDEBOOK

SPECIAL TOOLS 1
TIME-LINES OF GOALS & SUCCESSES: WEEKLY/MONTHLY/YEARS 1 TO 50

<u>YEARS 10 TO 15 (FROM CURRENT YEAR)</u>

GOALS:

_____

_____

_____

SUCCESSES:

_____

_____

_____

GOALS FROM PREVIOUS 5 YEARS (YEARS 5 – 10) MET? PROJECT, ENVISION & CONNECT.

_____

SOME DETAILS OF YOUR LIFE IN THESE LAST 5 YEARS (10 – 15 YEARS FORWARD FROM CURRENT):

_____

_____

_____

WARNING:
IF YOU WERE TO DIE THIS 5-YEAR PERIOD, BRIEFLY DECRIBE YOUR "EULOGY" OR BIOGRAPHY,
ESPECIALLY WHAT YOU ACCOMPLISHED AND WHAT LEGACY YOU LEFT BEHIND FOR OTHERS:

_____

_____

_____

21 Ps™

WORLD'S SUREST...FASTEST...SYSTEM FOR MONEY & SUCCESS...MLM CUSTOM GUIDEBOOK

SPECIAL TOOLS 1
TIME-LINES OF GOALS & SUCCESSES: WEEKLY/MONTHLY/YEARS 1 TO 50

<u>YEARS 5 TO 10 (FROM CURRENT YEAR)</u>

GOALS:

_____

_____

_____

SUCCESSES:

_____

_____

_____

GOALS FROM PREVIOUS 2 YEARS (YEARS 3– 5) MET? PROJECT, ENVISION & CONNECT.

_____

SOME DETAILS OF YOUR LIFE IN THESE LAST 5 YEARS (5 – 10 YEARS FORWARD FROM CURRENT):

_____

_____

_____

WARNING:
IF YOU WERE TO DIE THIS 5-YEAR PERIOD, BRIEFLY DECRIBE YOUR "EULOGY" OR BIOGRAPHY, ESPECIALLY WHAT YOU ACCOMPLISHED AND WHAT LEGACY YOU LEFT BEHIND FOR OTHERS:

_____

_____

_____

21 Ps™

WORLD'S SUREST...FASTEST...SYSTEM FOR MONEY & SUCCESS...MLM CUSTOM GUIDEBOOK

SPECIAL TOOLS 1
TIME-LINES OF GOALS & SUCCESSES: WEEKLY/MONTHLY/YEARS 1 TO 50

<u>YEARS 3 TO 5 (FROM CURRENT YEAR)</u>

GOALS:

_____

_____

_____

SUCCESSES:

_____

_____

_____

GOALS FROM PREVIOUS 2 YEARS (YEARS 1 – 3) MET? PROJECT, ENVISION & CONNECT.

_____

SOME DETAILS OF YOUR LIFE IN THESE LAST 2 YEARS (3 –5 YEARS FORWARD FROM CURRENT):

_____

_____

_____

WARNING:
IF YOU WERE TO DIE THIS 2-YEAR PERIOD, BRIEFLY DECRIBE YOUR "EULOGY" OR BIOGRAPHY,
ESPECIALLY WHAT YOU ACCOMPLISHED AND WHAT LEGACY YOU LEFT BEHIND FOR OTHERS:

_____

_____

_____

21 Ps™

WORLD'S SUREST...FASTEST...SYSTEM FOR MONEY & SUCCESS...MLM CUSTOM GUIDEBOOK

SPECIAL TOOLS 1
TIME-LINES OF GOALS & SUCCESSES: WEEKLY/MONTHLY/YEARS 1 TO 50

<u>YEARS 1 TO 3 (FROM CURRENT YEAR)</u>

GOALS:

_____

_____

_____

SUCCESSES:

_____

_____

_____

GOALS FROM PREVIOUS YEAR (YEAR 0 – 1) MET? PROJECT, ENVISION & CONNECT.

_____

SOME DETAILS OF YOUR LIFE IN THESE LAST 2 YEARS (1 –3 YEARS FORWARD FROM CURRENT):

_____

_____

_____

WARNING:
IF YOU WERE TO DIE THIS 2-YEAR PERIOD, BRIEFLY DECRIBE YOUR "EULOGY" OR BIOGRAPHY, ESPECIALLY WHAT YOU ACCOMPLISHED AND WHAT LEGACY YOU LEFT BEHIND FOR OTHERS:

_____

_____

_____

21 Ps™

WORLD'S SUREST...FASTEST...SYSTEM FOR MONEY & SUCCESS...MLM CUSTOM GUIDEBOOK

SPECIAL TOOLS 1
TIME-LINES OF GOALS & SUCCESSES: WEEKLY/MONTHLY/YEARS 1 TO 50

<u>THIS COMING YEAR (FROM PRESENT)</u>

GOALS:

_____

_____

_____

SUCCESSES SO FAR:

_____

_____

_____

GOALS FROM PREVIOUS 2 YEARS MET?

_____

SOME DETAILS OF YOUR LIFE NOW:

_____

_____

_____

SEVERE WARNING:
IF YOU WERE TO DIE THIS YEAR, BRIEFLY DECRIBE YOUR "EULOGY" OR BIOGRAPHY, ESPECIALLY
WHAT YOU HAVE ACCOMPLISHED AND WHAT LEGACY YOU HAVE LEFT BEHIND FOR OTHERS:

_____

_____

_____

21 Ps™

WORLD'S SUREST...FASTEST...SYSTEM FOR MONEY & SUCCESS...MLM CUSTOM GUIDEBOOK

SPECIAL TOOLS 1
TIME-LINES OF GOALS & SUCCESSES: WEEKLY/MONTHLY/YEARS 1 TO 50

<u>MONTH 1 OF 6</u>
(START FROM ANY MONTH & GO FORWARD)

Weekly Small Goals/Successes:

_____

_____

_____

_____

_____

BIG GOAL
Deadline This Month?

Success(es) This Month
Re: BIG Goal:

_____

_____

_____

MONTHLY TRAINING
List at Least
3 Ps Focused On:

_____

_____

_____

_____

If 30-Day "SUDU"
(Super Duplication) Drive:
Do <u>ALL</u> 15 Ps in 3 Book Sections

Week One (Priorities/Events/Appointments):

_____

_____

_____

Week Two (Priorities/Events/Appointments):

_____

_____

_____

Week Three (Priorities/Events/Appointments):

_____

_____

_____

Week Four (Priorities/Events/Appointments):

_____

_____

_____

Week Five (Priorities/Events/Appointments):

_____

_____

_____

21 Ps™

WORLD'S SUREST...FASTEST...SYSTEM FOR MONEY & SUCCESS...MLM CUSTOM GUIDEBOOK

SPECIAL TOOLS 1
TIME-LINES OF GOALS & SUCCESSES: WEEKLY/MONTHLY/YEARS 1 TO 50

<u>MONTH 2 OF 6</u>
(START FROM ANY MONTH & GO FORWARD)

Weekly Small Goals/Successes:	Week One (Priorities/Events/Appointments):
_____	_____
_____	_____
_____	Week Two (Priorities/Events/Appointments):
_____	_____
_____	_____
BIG GOAL Deadline This Month?	_____
Success(es) This Month Re: BIG Goal:	Week Three (Priorities/Events/Appointments):
_____	_____
_____	_____
_____	_____
MONTHLY TRAINING List at Least 3 Ps Focused On:	Week Four (Priorities/Events/Appointments):
_____	_____
_____	_____
_____	Week Five (Priorities/Events/Appointments):
_____	_____
If 30-Day "SUDU" (Super Duplication) Drive: Do <u>ALL</u> 15 Ps in 3 Book Sections	_____

21 Ps™

WORLD'S SUREST...FASTEST...SYSTEM FOR MONEY & SUCCESS...MLM CUSTOM GUIDEBOOK

SPECIAL TOOLS 1
TIME-LINES OF GOALS & SUCCESSES: WEEKLY/MONTHLY/YEARS 1 TO 50

MONTH 3 OF 6
(START FROM ANY MONTH & GO FORWARD)

Weekly Small Goals/Successes:	Week One (Priorities/Events/Appointments):
	Week Two (Priorities/Events/Appointments):
BIG GOAL Deadline This Month?	
Success(es) This Month Re: BIG Goal:	Week Three (Priorities/Events/Appointments):
MONTHLY TRAINING List at Least 3 Ps Focused On:	Week Four (Priorities/Events/Appointments):
	Week Five (Priorities/Events/Appointments):
If 30-Day "SUDU" (Super Duplication) Drive: Do ALL 15 Ps in 3 Book Sections	

21 Ps™

WORLD'S SUREST...FASTEST...SYSTEM FOR MONEY & SUCCESS...MLM CUSTOM GUIDEBOOK

SPECIAL TOOLS 1
TIME-LINES OF GOALS & SUCCESSES: WEEKLY/MONTHLY/YEARS 1 TO 50

<u>MONTH 4 OF 6</u>
(START FROM ANY MONTH & GO FORWARD)

Weekly Small Goals/Successes:	Week One (Priorities/Events/Appointments):
_____	_____
_____	_____
_____	
	Week Two (Priorities/Events/Appointments):
_____	_____
_____	_____
BIG GOAL Deadline This Month?	_____
Success(es) This Month Re: BIG Goal:	Week Three (Priorities/Events/Appointments):
_____	_____
_____	_____
_____	_____
MONTHLY TRAINING List at Least 3 Ps Focused On:	Week Four (Priorities/Events/Appointments):
_____	_____
_____	_____
_____	_____
_____	Week Five (Priorities/Events/Appointments):
	_____
If 30-Day "SUDU" (Super Duplication) Drive: Do <u>ALL</u> 15 Ps in 3 Book Sections	_____
	_____

21 Ps™

WORLD'S SUREST...FASTEST...SYSTEM FOR MONEY & SUCCESS...MLM CUSTOM GUIDEBOOK

SPECIAL TOOLS 1
TIME-LINES OF GOALS & SUCCESSES: WEEKLY/MONTHLY/YEARS 1 TO 50

Weekly Small Goals/Successes:	Week One (Priorities/Events/Appointments):
_____	_____
_____	_____
_____	
_____	Week Two (Priorities/Events/Appointments):
_____	_____
BIG GOAL Deadline This Month?	_____
Success(es) This Month Re: BIG Goal:	_____
_____	Week Three (Priorities/Events/Appointments):
_____	_____
_____	_____
MONTHLY TRAINING List at Least 3 Ps Focused On:	Week Four (Priorities/Events/Appointments):
_____	_____
_____	_____
_____	_____
_____	Week Five (Priorities/Events/Appointments):
_____	_____
If 30-Day "SUDU" (Super Duplication) Drive: Do <u>ALL</u> 15 Ps in 3 Book Sections	_____

21 Ps™

WORLD'S SUREST...FASTEST...SYSTEM FOR MONEY & SUCCESS...MLM CUSTOM GUIDEBOOK

SPECIAL TOOLS 1
TIME-LINES OF GOALS & SUCCESSES: WEEKLY/MONTHLY/YEARS 1 TO 50

Weekly Small Goals/Successes:

_____

_____

_____

_____

_____

BIG GOAL
Deadline This Month?

Success(es) This Month
Re: BIG Goal:

_____

_____

_____

MONTHLY TRAINING
List at Least
3 Ps Focused On:

_____

_____

_____

_____

If 30-Day "SUDU"
(Super Duplication) Drive:
Do ALL 15 Ps in 3 Book Sections

Week One (Priorities/Events/Appointments):

_____

_____

Week Two (Priorities/Events/Appointments):

_____

_____

_____

Week Three (Priorities/Events/Appointments):

_____

_____

Week Four (Priorities/Events/Appointments):

_____

_____

_____

Week Five (Priorities/Events/Appointments):

_____

_____

_____

21 Ps™
WORLD'S SUREST...FASTEST...SYSTEM FOR MONEY & SUCCESS...MLM CUSTOM GUIDEBOOK

BLANK PAGE

SPECIAL TOOL 2

PROSPECTING-PARTNERING DATABASE / SPECIAL LISTS

FOLLOWING ARE LISTS THAT A REPRESENTATIVE USES TO BUILD A TEAM. THESE LISTS FORM THE EXPANDING AND REFINED DATABASE THAT CONSISTS OF THE REPRESENTATIVE'S SPHERES OF INFLUENCE AND LISTS DEVELOPED THROUGH THE PROSPECTING-PARTNERSHIP SKILLS AND TECHNIQUES DISCUSSED IN CHAPTER 11.

PARTICULARLY IMPORTANT ARE REFERRAL LISTS, SOCIAL NETWORKING LISTS AND OTHER LISTS BUILT UP FROM CREATIVE MARKETING. DEPENDING ON CIRCUMSTANCE AND COMFORT LEVEL, A REPRESENTATIVE CAN APPROACH HIS OR HER "WARM" MARKET SOONER OR LATER. IF SOMEONE IS STARTING TO GET POSITIVE MLM RESULTS, "WARM" MARKETS GET MUCH "WARMER". SUCCESS BREEDS SUCCESS!

21 Ps™

WORLD'S SUREST...FASTEST...SYSTEM FOR MONEY & SUCCESS...MLM CUSTOM GUIDEBOOK

BLANK PAGE FOR

SPECIAL TOOLS 2

NOTES

21 Ps™

WORLD'S SUREST...FASTEST...SYSTEM FOR MONEY & SUCCESS...MLM CUSTOM GUIDEBOOK

SPECIAL TOOLS 2
PROSPECTING-PARTNERING DATABASE / SPECIAL LISTS

"WARM MARKET" PROSPECTING-PARTNERING LIST
-Fill in as completely/diligently as possible-

Date of Initial Contact: _____
Name:

Address:

Phone:

Email:

Prospect's Own Website or Special Group/Affiliation:

Dates of Additional Contacts: _____

SPECIAL NOTES
Business or Occupation:

Note also above if Prospect has been to a Presentation, uses any of the MLM Products or Services or is new to MLM; Rate on a scale from 1 to 5 this Prospect's Level of Interest: 1 = Not interested to 5 = Ready to Sign up

===

Date of Initial Contact: _____
Name:

Address:

Phone:

Email:

Prospect's Own Website or Special Group/Affiliation:

Dates of Additional Contacts: _____

SPECIAL NOTES
Business or Occupation:

Note also above if Prospect has been to a Presentation, uses any of the MLM Products or Services or is new to MLM; Rate on a scale from 1 to 5 this Prospect's Level of Interest: 1=Not interested to 5=Ready to Sign up

You can make multiple copies of this Page. Attach any additional Pages to this Section for convenience and organization.

21 Ps™

WORLD'S SUREST...FASTEST...SYSTEM FOR MONEY & SUCCESS...MLM CUSTOM GUIDEBOOK

SPECIAL TOOLS 2
PROSPECTING-PARTNERING DATABASE / SPECIAL LISTS

"WARM MARKET" PROSPECTING-PARTNERING LIST
-Fill in as completely/diligently as possible-

Date of Initial Contact: _____
Name:

_____

Address:

_____

_____

Phone:
_____

Email:
_____

Prospect's Own Website or Special Group/Affiliation:
_____

Dates of Additional Contacts: _____
_____

SPECIAL NOTES
Business or Occupation:

_____

_____

_____

_____

_____

_____

Note also above if Prospect has been to a Presentation, uses any of the MLM Products or Services or is new to MLM; Rate on a scale from 1 to 5 this Prospect's Level of Interest: 1 = Not interested to 5 = Ready to Sign up

_____

==

Date of Initial Contact: _____
Name:

_____

Address:

_____

_____

Phone:
_____

Email:
_____

Prospect's Own Website or Special Group/Affiliation:
_____

Dates of Additional Contacts: _____
_____

SPECIAL NOTES
Business or Occupation:

_____

_____

_____

_____

_____

_____

Note also above if Prospect has been to a Presentation, uses any of the MLM Products or Services or is new to MLM; Rate on a scale from 1 to 5 this Prospect's Level of Interest: 1=Not interested to 5=Ready to Sign up

_____

You can make multiple copies of this Page. Attach any additional Pages to this Section for convenience and organization.

21 Ps™

WORLD'S SUREST...FASTEST...SYSTEM FOR MONEY & SUCCESS...MLM CUSTOM GUIDEBOOK

SPECIAL TOOLS 2
PROSPECTING-PARTNERING DATABASE / SPECIAL LISTS

"WARM MARKET" PROSPECTING-PARTNERING LIST
-Fill in as completely/diligently as possible-

Date of Initial Contact: _____
Name:

_____

Address:

_____

_____

Phone:
_____

Email:
_____

Prospect's Own Website or Special Group/Affiliation:
_____

Dates of Additional Contacts: _____
_____

SPECIAL NOTES
Business or Occupation:

_____

_____

_____

_____

_____

_____

Note also above if Prospect has been to a Presentation, uses any of the MLM Products or Services or is new to MLM; Rate on a scale from 1 to 5 this Prospect's Level of Interest:
1 = Not interested to 5 = Ready to Sign up

_____

===

Date of Initial Contact: _____
Name:

_____

Address:

_____

_____

Phone:
_____

Email:
_____

Prospect's Own Website or Special Group/Affiliation:
_____

Dates of Additional Contacts: _____
_____

SPECIAL NOTES
Business or Occupation:

_____

_____

_____

_____

_____

_____

Note also above if Prospect has been to a Presentation, uses any of the MLM Products or Services or is new to MLM; Rate on a scale from 1 to 5 this Prospect's Level of Interest:
1=Not interested to 5=Ready to Sign up

_____

You can make multiple copies of this Page. Attach any additional Pages to this Section for convenience and organization.

21 Ps™

WORLD'S SUREST...FASTEST...SYSTEM FOR MONEY & SUCCESS...MLM CUSTOM GUIDEBOOK

SPECIAL TOOLS 2
PROSPECTING-PARTNERING DATABASE / SPECIAL LISTS

"WARM MARKET" PROSPECTING-PARTNERING LIST
-Fill in as completely/diligently as possible-

Date of Initial Contact: _____
Name:

_____

Address:

_____

_____

Phone:

_____

Email:

_____
Prospect's Own Website or Special Group/Affiliation:

_____

Dates of Additional Contacts: _____

_____

SPECIAL NOTES
Business or Occupation:

_____

_____

_____

_____

_____

_____

Note also above if Prospect has been to a Presentation, uses any of the MLM Products or Services or is new to MLM; Rate on a scale from 1 to 5 this Prospect's Level of Interest: 1 = Not interested to 5 = Ready to Sign up

_____

===

Date of Initial Contact: _____
Name:

_____

Address:

_____

_____

Phone:

_____

Email:

_____
Prospect's Own Website or Special Group/Affiliation:

_____

Dates of Additional Contacts: _____

_____

SPECIAL NOTES
Business or Occupation:

_____

_____

_____

_____

_____

_____

Note also above if Prospect has been to a Presentation, uses any of the MLM Products or Services or is new to MLM; Rate on a scale from 1 to 5 this Prospect's Level of Interest: 1=Not interested to 5=Ready to Sign up

_____

You can make multiple copies of this Page. Attach any additional Pages to this Section for convenience and organization.

21 Ps™

WORLD'S SUREST...FASTEST...SYSTEM FOR MONEY & SUCCESS...MLM CUSTOM GUIDEBOOK

SPECIAL TOOLS 2
PROSPECTING-PARTNERING DATABASE / SPECIAL LISTS

REFERRALS LIST
-Fill in as completely/diligently as possible-

Referred By: _____
Name:

SPECIAL NOTES
Business or Occupation:

_____

Address:

_____

_____

_____

Phone:

_____

Email:

_____

Prospect's Own Website or Special Group/Affiliation:

Note also above if Prospect has been to a Presentation, uses any of the MLM Products or Services or is new to MLM; Rate on a scale from 1 to 5 this Prospect's Level of Interest:

Dates of Contacts: _____

1 = Not interested to 5 = Ready to Sign up

_____

==

Referred By: _____
Name:

SPECIAL NOTES
Business or Occupation:

_____

Address:

_____

_____

_____

Phone:

_____

Email:

_____

Prospect's Own Website or Special Group/Affiliation:

Note also above if Prospect has been to a Presentation, uses any of the MLM Products or Services or is new to MLM; Rate on a scale from 1 to 5 this Prospect's Level of Interest:

Dates of Contacts: _____

1=Not interested to 5=Ready to Sign up

_____

You can make multiple copies of this Page. Attach any additional Pages to this Section for convenience and organization.

21 Ps™

WORLD'S SUREST...FASTEST...SYSTEM FOR MONEY & SUCCESS...MLM CUSTOM GUIDEBOOK

SPECIAL TOOLS 2
PROSPECTING-PARTNERING DATABASE / SPECIAL LISTS

REFERRALS LIST
-Fill in as completely/diligently as possible-

Referred By: _____
Name:

_____

Address:

_____

_____

Phone:

_____

Email:

_____

Prospect's Own Website or Special Group/Affiliation:

_____

Dates of Contacts: _____

_____

SPECIAL NOTES
Business or Occupation:

_____

_____

_____

_____

_____

Note also above if Prospect has been to a Presentation, uses any of the MLM Products or Services or is new to MLM; Rate on a scale from 1 to 5 this Prospect's Level of Interest: 1 = Not interested to 5 = Ready to Sign up

_____

==

Referred By: _____
Name:

_____

Address:

_____

_____

Phone:

_____

Email:

_____

Prospect's Own Website or Special Group/Affiliation:

_____

Dates of Contacts: _____

_____

SPECIAL NOTES
Business or Occupation:

_____

_____

_____

_____

_____

Note also above if Prospect has been to a Presentation, uses any of the MLM Products or Services or is new to MLM; Rate on a scale from 1 to 5 this Prospect's Level of Interest: 1=Not interested to 5=Ready to Sign up

_____

You can make multiple copies of this Page. Attach any additional Pages to this Section for convenience and organization.

21 Ps™

WORLD'S SUREST...FASTEST...SYSTEM FOR MONEY & SUCCESS...MLM CUSTOM GUIDEBOOK

SPECIAL TOOLS 2
PROSPECTING-PARTNERING DATABASE / SPECIAL LISTS

REFERRALS LIST
-Fill in as completely/diligently as possible-

Referred By: _____

Name: _____

Address: _____

_____

Phone: _____

Email: _____

Prospect's Own Website or Special Group/Affiliation:

_____

Dates of Contacts: _____

_____

SPECIAL NOTES
Business or Occupation:

_____

_____

_____

_____

_____

_____

Note also above if Prospect has been to a Presentation, uses any of the MLM Products or Services or is new to MLM; Rate on a scale from 1 to 5 this Prospect's Level of Interest: 1 = Not interested to 5 = Ready to Sign up

_____

===

Referred By: _____

Name: _____

Address: _____

_____

Phone: _____

Email: _____

Prospect's Own Website or Special Group/Affiliation:

_____

Dates of Contacts: _____

_____

SPECIAL NOTES
Business or Occupation:

_____

_____

_____

_____

_____

_____

Note also above if Prospect has been to a Presentation, uses any of the MLM Products or Services or is new to MLM; Rate on a scale from 1 to 5 this Prospect's Level of Interest: 1=Not interested to 5=Ready to Sign up

_____

You can make multiple copies of this Page. Attach any additional Pages to this Section for convenience and organization.

21 Ps™

WORLD'S SUREST...FASTEST...SYSTEM FOR MONEY & SUCCESS...MLM CUSTOM GUIDEBOOK

SPECIAL TOOLS 2
PROSPECTING-PARTNERING DATABASE / SPECIAL LISTS

REFERRALS LIST
-Fill in as completely/diligently as possible-

Referred By: _____

Name:

_____

Address:

_____

_____

Phone:

_____

Email:

_____

Prospect's Own Website or Special Group/Affiliation:

_____

Dates of Contacts: _____

_____

SPECIAL NOTES
Business or Occupation:

_____

_____

_____

_____

_____

_____

Note also above if Prospect has been to a Presentation, uses any of the MLM Products or Services or is new to MLM; Rate on a scale from 1 to 5 this Prospect's Level of Interest: 1 = Not interested to 5 = Ready to Sign up

_____

===

Referred By: _____

Name:

_____

Address:

_____

_____

Phone:

_____

Email:

_____

Prospect's Own Website or Special Group/Affiliation:

_____

Dates of Contacts: _____

_____

SPECIAL NOTES
Business or Occupation:

_____

_____

_____

_____

_____

_____

Note also above if Prospect has been to a Presentation, uses any of the MLM Products or Services or is new to MLM; Rate on a scale from 1 to 5 this Prospect's Level of Interest: 1=Not interested to 5=Ready to Sign up

_____

You can make multiple copies of this Page. Attach any additional Pages to this Section for convenience and organization.

21 Ps™

WORLD'S SUREST...FASTEST...SYSTEM FOR MONEY & SUCCESS...MLM CUSTOM GUIDEBOOK

SPECIAL TOOLS 2
PROSPECTING-PARTNERING DATABASE / SPECIAL LISTS

INTERNET SOCIAL/BUSINESS NETWORKING LIST
-Fill in as completely/diligently as possible-

Social/Business Net Site: _____
Name:

SPECIAL NOTES
Business or Occupation:

Address:

Phone:

Email:

Prospect's Own Website or Special Group/Affiliation:

Note also above if Prospect has been to a Presentation, uses any of the MLM Products or Services or is new to MLM; Rate on a scale from 1 to 5 this Prospect's Level of Interest:

Dates of Contacts: _____

1 = Not interested to 5 = Ready to Sign up

==

Social/Business Net Site: _____
Name:

SPECIAL NOTES
Business or Occupation:

Address:

Phone:

Email:

Prospect's Own Website or Special Group/Affiliation:

Note also above if Prospect has been to a Presentation, uses any of the MLM Products or Services or is new to MLM; Rate on a scale from 1 to 5 this Prospect's Level of Interest:

Dates of Contacts: _____

1=Not interested to 5=Ready to Sign up

You can make multiple copies of this Page. Attach any additional Pages to this Section for convenience and organization.

21 Ps™

WORLD'S SUREST...FASTEST...SYSTEM FOR MONEY & SUCCESS...MLM CUSTOM GUIDEBOOK

SPECIAL TOOLS 2
PROSPECTING-PARTNERING DATABASE / SPECIAL LISTS

INTERNET SOCIAL/BUSINESS NETWORKING LIST
-Fill in as completely/diligently as possible-

Social/Business Net Site: _____
Name:

_____

Address:

_____

_____

Phone:

_____

Email:

_____

Prospect's Own Website or Special Group/Affiliation:

_____

Dates of Contacts: _____

_____

SPECIAL NOTES
Business or Occupation:

_____

_____

_____

_____

_____

Note also above if Prospect has been to a Presentation, uses any of the MLM Products or Services or is new to MLM; Rate on a scale from 1 to 5 this Prospect's Level of Interest: 1 = Not interested to 5 = Ready to Sign up

_____

===

Social/Business Net Site: _____
Name:

_____

Address:

_____

_____

Phone:

_____

Email:

_____

Prospect's Own Website or Special Group/Affiliation:

_____

Dates of Contacts: _____

_____

SPECIAL NOTES
Business or Occupation:

_____

_____

_____

_____

_____

Note also above if Prospect has been to a Presentation, uses any of the MLM Products or Services or is new to MLM; Rate on a scale from 1 to 5 this Prospect's Level of Interest: 1=Not interested to 5=Ready to Sign up

_____

You can make multiple copies of this Page. Attach any additional Pages to this Section for convenience and organization.

21 Ps™

WORLD'S SUREST...FASTEST...SYSTEM FOR MONEY & SUCCESS...MLM CUSTOM GUIDEBOOK

SPECIAL TOOLS 2
PROSPECTING-PARTNERING DATABASE / SPECIAL LISTS

INTERNET SOCIAL/BUSINESS NETWORKING LIST
-Fill in as completely/diligently as possible-

Social/Business Net Site: _____
Name:

_____

Address:

_____

_____

Phone:
_____

Email:
_____

Prospect's Own Website or Special Group/Affiliation:
_____

Dates of Contacts: _____

_____

SPECIAL NOTES
Business or Occupation:

_____

_____

_____

_____

_____

_____

Note also above if Prospect has been to a Presentation, uses any of the MLM Products or Services or is new to MLM; Rate on a scale from 1 to 5 this Prospect's Level of Interest: 1 = Not interested to 5 = Ready to Sign up

_____

==

Social/Business Net Site: _____
Name:

_____

Address:

_____

_____

Phone:
_____

Email:
_____

Prospect's Own Website or Special Group/Affiliation:
_____

Dates of Contacts: _____

_____

SPECIAL NOTES
Business or Occupation:

_____

_____

_____

_____

_____

_____

Note also above if Prospect has been to a Presentation, uses any of the MLM Products or Services or is new to MLM; Rate on a scale from 1 to 5 this Prospect's Level of Interest: 1=Not interested to 5=Ready to Sign up

_____

You can make multiple copies of this Page. Attach any additional Pages to this Section for convenience and organization.

21 Ps™

WORLD'S SUREST...FASTEST...SYSTEM FOR MONEY & SUCCESS...MLM CUSTOM GUIDEBOOK

SPECIAL TOOLS 2
PROSPECTING-PARTNERING DATABASE / SPECIAL LISTS

INTERNET SOCIAL/BUSINESS NETWORKING LIST
-Fill in as completely/diligently as possible-

Social/Business Net Site: _____
Name:

_____

Address:

_____

_____

Phone:

_____

Email:

_____

Prospect's Own Website or Special Group/Affiliation:

_____

Dates of Contacts: _____

_____

SPECIAL NOTES
Business or Occupation:

_____

_____

_____

_____

_____

Note also above if Prospect has been to a Presentation, uses any of the MLM Products or Services or is new to MLM; Rate on a scale from 1 to 5 this Prospect's Level of Interest: 1 = Not interested to 5 = Ready to Sign up

_____

===

Social/Business Net Site: _____
Name:

_____

Address:

_____

_____

Phone:

_____

Email:

_____

Prospect's Own Website or Special Group/Affiliation:

_____

Dates of Contacts: _____

_____

SPECIAL NOTES
Business or Occupation:

_____

_____

_____

_____

_____

Note also above if Prospect has been to a Presentation, uses any of the MLM Products or Services or is new to MLM; Rate on a scale from 1 to 5 this Prospect's Level of Interest: 1=Not interested to 5=Ready to Sign up

_____

You can make multiple copies of this Page. Attach any additional Pages to this Section for convenience and organization.

SPECIAL TOOLS 3

PROFILES
OF
<u>YOUR</u> EXPANDING GROUP OF
MLM LEADERS

THE PRODUCTIVE RESULTS OF YOUR PROSPECTING HAS BROUGHT RECRUITS UNDER YOU. YOU NOW HAVE A DOWNLINE AND ARE BUILDING YOUR ORGANIZATION!

HOW YOUR RECRUITS BECOME LEADERS IS THE KEY TO YOUR SUCCESS, YOUR TEAM'S AND THE OVERALL MLM COMPANY'S.

THE FOLLOWING FORMS ALLOW YOU TO PROFILE YOUR MLM LEADERS.

YOU NEED TO ASCERTAIN INFORMATION AND DATA. YOU NEED TO OBSERVE, MEASURE AND ASSESS SO THAT WEAKNESSES CAN BE MINIMIZED AND STRENGTHS AMPLIFIED.

YOU CAN DISCOVER WHAT TO TRAIN, TEACH AND CULTIVATE IN YOUR LEADERS AS YOU IN TURN ENHANCE YOUR LEADERSHIP SKILLS, ATTITUDES AND ABILITIES.

21 Ps™

WORLD'S SUREST...FASTEST...SYSTEM FOR MONEY & SUCCESS...MLM CUSTOM GUIDEBOOK

BLANK PAGE FOR

SPECIAL TOOLS 3

NOTES

21 Ps™

WORLD'S SUREST...FASTEST...SYSTEM FOR MONEY & SUCCESS...MLM CUSTOM GUIDEBOOK

SPECIAL TOOLS 3
PROFILES OF <u>YOUR</u> EXPANDING GROUP OF MLM LEADERS

<u>LEADER PROFILES</u>

BASICS & DATA	SELF-ASSESSMENTS & SPONSOR'S
Name: _____	Knowledge of MLM Products or Services: _____ _____
Phone: _____	
Address: _____ _____	Coachability and Trainability: _____ _____
Email: _____	Prospecting Skills: _____ _____
Date of Sign-up: _____	
"Fast-Start" Completed? _____	
# of 2-on-1 Appointments: _____	Leadership Skills: _____ _____
# of Solo Appointments: _____	
# of Home Presentations Conducted: _____	Miscellaneous Notes Re: Purpose, Motivation, Energy and Special Talents: _____ _____
Group Presentation Participation: _____	_____
Interested in 30-Day SUDU (Super Duplication) Drive? _____	_____

BOTTOM LINE:	BOTTOM LINES (Personal / Group Volumes):	
Names of New Recruits: _____ _____ _____ _____ _____	Month 1: _____	Month 2: _____
	Month 3: _____	Month 4: _____
	Month 5: _____	Month 6: _____
	Month 7: _____	Month 8: _____
	Month 9: _____	Month 10: _____
	Month 11: _____	Month 12: _____

You can make multiple copies of this Page. Attach any additional Pages to this Section for convenience and organization.

21 Ps™

WORLD'S SUREST...FASTEST...SYSTEM FOR MONEY & SUCCESS...MLM CUSTOM GUIDEBOOK

SPECIAL TOOLS 3
PROFILES OF <u>YOUR</u> EXPANDING GROUP OF MLM LEADERS

<u>LEADER PROFILES</u>

BASICS & DATA	SELF-ASSESSMENTS & SPONSOR'S
Name:	Knowledge of MLM Products or Services:
Phone:	
Address:	Coachability and Trainability:
Email:	Prospecting Skills:
Date of Sign-up:	
"Fast-Start" Completed?	
# of 2-on-1 Appointments:	Leadership Skills:
# of Solo Appointments:	
# of Home Presentations Conducted:	Miscellaneous Notes Re: Purpose, Motivation, Energy and Special Talents:
Group Presentation Participation:	
Interested in 30-Day SUDU (Super Duplication) Drive?	

BOTTOM LINE:	BOTTOM LINES (Personal / Group Volumes):
Names of New Recruits:	Month 1: _____ Month 2: _____
	Month 3: _____ Month 4: _____
	Month 5: _____ Month 6: _____
	Month 7: _____ Month 8: _____
	Month 9: _____ Month 10: _____
	Month 11: _____ Month 12: _____

You can make multiple copies of this Page. Attach any additional Pages to this Section for convenience and organization.

21 Ps™

WORLD'S SUREST...FASTEST...SYSTEM FOR MONEY & SUCCESS...MLM CUSTOM GUIDEBOOK

SPECIAL TOOLS 3
PROFILES OF <u>YOUR</u> EXPANDING GROUP OF MLM LEADERS

<u>LEADER PROFILES</u>

BASICS & DATA	SELF-ASSESSMENTS & SPONSOR'S
Name:	Knowledge of MLM Products or Services:
Phone:	
Address:	Coachability and Trainability:
Email:	Prospecting Skills:
Date of Sign-up:	
"Fast-Start" Completed?	
# of 2-on-1 Appointments:	Leadership Skills:
# of Solo Appointments:	
# of Home Presentations Conducted:	Miscellaneous Notes Re: Purpose, Motivation, Energy and Special Talents:
Group Presentation Participation:	
Interested in 30-Day SUDU (Super Duplication) Drive?	

BOTTOM LINE:	BOTTOM LINES (Personal / Group Volumes):
Names of New Recruits:	Month 1: _____ Month 2: _____
	Month 3: _____ Month 4: _____
	Month 5: _____ Month 6: _____
	Month 7: _____ Month 8: _____
	Month 9: _____ Month 10: _____
	Month 11: _____ Month 12: _____

You can make multiple copies of this Page. Attach any additional Pages to this Section for convenience and organization.

21 Ps™

WORLD'S SUREST...FASTEST...SYSTEM FOR MONEY & SUCCESS...MLM CUSTOM GUIDEBOOK

SPECIAL TOOLS 3
PROFILES OF <u>YOUR</u> EXPANDING GROUP OF MLM LEADERS

<u>LEADER PROFILES</u>

BASICS & DATA	SELF-ASSESSMENTS & SPONSOR'S
Name:	Knowledge of MLM Products or Services:
Phone:	
Address:	Coachability and Trainability:
Email:	Prospecting Skills:
Date of Sign-up:	
"Fast-Start" Completed?	
# of 2-on-1 Appointments:	Leadership Skills:
# of Solo Appointments:	
# of Home Presentations Conducted:	Miscellaneous Notes Re: Purpose, Motivation, Energy and Special Talents:
Group Presentation Participation:	
Interested in 30-Day SUDU (Super Duplication) Drive?	

BOTTOM LINE:	BOTTOM LINES (Personal / Group Volumes):	
Names of New Recruits:	Month 1: _____	Month 2: _____
	Month 3: _____	Month 4: _____
	Month 5: _____	Month 6: _____
	Month 7: _____	Month 8: _____
	Month 9: _____	Month 10: _____
	Month 11: _____	Month 12: _____

You can make multiple copies of this Page. Attach any additional Pages to this Section for convenience and organization.

21 Ps™

WORLD'S SUREST...FASTEST...SYSTEM FOR MONEY & SUCCESS...MLM CUSTOM GUIDEBOOK

<u>LEADER PROFILES</u>

BASICS & DATA	SELF-ASSESSMENTS & SPONSOR'S
Name:	Knowledge of MLM Products or Services:
Phone:	
Address:	Coachability and Trainability:
Email:	Prospecting Skills:
Date of Sign-up:	
"Fast-Start" Completed?	
# of 2-on-1 Appointments:	Leadership Skills:
# of Solo Appointments:	
# of Home Presentations Conducted:	Miscellaneous Notes Re: Purpose, Motivation, Energy and Special Talents:
Group Presentation Participation:	
Interested in 30-Day SUDU (Super Duplication) Drive?	

BOTTOM LINE:	BOTTOM LINES (Personal / Group Volumes):	
Names of New Recruits:	Month 1: _____	Month 2: _____
	Month 3: _____	Month 4: _____
	Month 5: _____	Month 6: _____
	Month 7: _____	Month 8: _____
	Month 9: _____	Month 10: _____
	Month 11: _____	Month 12: _____

You can make multiple copies of this Page. Attach any additional Pages to this Section for convenience and organization.

21 Ps™

WORLD'S SUREST...FASTEST...SYSTEM FOR MONEY & SUCCESS...MLM CUSTOM GUIDEBOOK

SPECIAL TOOLS 3
PROFILES OF <u>YOUR</u> EXPANDING GROUP OF MLM LEADERS

<u>LEADER PROFILES</u>

BASICS & DATA	SELF-ASSESSMENTS & SPONSOR'S
Name:	Knowledge of MLM Products or Services:
Phone:	
Address:	Coachability and Trainability:
Email:	Prospecting Skills:
Date of Sign-up:	
"Fast-Start" Completed?	Leadership Skills:
# of 2-on-1 Appointments:	
# of Solo Appointments:	
# of Home Presentations Conducted:	Miscellaneous Notes Re: Purpose, Motivation, Energy and Special Talents:
Group Presentation Participation:	
Interested in 30-Day SUDU (Super Duplication) Drive?	

BOTTOM LINE:	BOTTOM LINES (Personal / Group Volumes):	
Names of New Recruits:	Month 1: _____	Month 2: _____
	Month 3: _____	Month 4: _____
	Month 5: _____	Month 6: _____
	Month 7: _____	Month 8: _____
	Month 9: _____	Month 10: _____
	Month 11: _____	Month 12: _____

You can make multiple copies of this Page. Attach any additional Pages to this Section for convenience and organization.

SPECIAL TOOLS 4

CREATIVE MARKETING /

"SUDU" (SUPER DUPLICATION) 30-DAY DRIVES

WITHIN THE MLM DUPLICATION SYSTEM AND IN SUPPORT OF IT, CREATIVE MARKETING IS THE APPLICATION OF INNOVATIVE AND IMAGINATIVE WAYS TO FIND CUSTOMERS AND APPROACH PROSPECTS IN BOTH ORDINARY PLACES AND UNUSUAL VENUES. THE SKILLED MLM REPRESENTATIVE NEEDS TO HAVE A CONSISTENT PROGRAM OF STEPS AND ACTIONS PRACTICED WITH CONVICTION AND INTENSITY.

THE "SUDU" (SUPER DUPLICATION) DRIVE IS A 30-DAY INTENSIVE CAMPAIGN THAT WILL GREATLY UPGRADE ALL THE SKILLS OF NETWORK MARKETING PRACTITIONERS AND DELIVER EXTRAORDINARY RESULTS, IF ONLY FOR ITS CREATION OF EXCITEMENT, URGENCY AND MASSIVENESS OF EFFORT.

21 Ps™

WORLD'S SUREST...FASTEST...SYSTEM FOR MONEY & SUCCESS...MLM CUSTOM GUIDEBOOK

SPECIAL TOOLS 4
CREATIVE MARKETING / "SUDU" (SUPER DUPLICATION) 30-DAY DRIVES

CREATIVE MARKETING

In addition to "ordinary" Prospecting strategies such as approaching your "Warm Market" and perhaps indiscriminately emailing your social network "Friends" on Facebook or adding to your profile on LinkedIn, there are many more ways to market yourself and your great products and opportunity, both old-school and high tech (maximizing the effectiveness of such venues as Facebook, LinkedIn and Twitter). Just a few ideas and examples below:

Joint Marketing or Cooperative Advertising with Businesses:

Non-competing businesses are usually open to joint marketing with fellow business-owners (such as the MLM business-person) where target customers can be exposed to mutual offerings and any advertising costs shared. Neighborhood enterprises are especially open to ideas to additional profit streams that the MLM products or services might generate. Additionally the business owner approached just might see the value of the MLM opportunity itself. Small shop owners tend to be risk-takers and ambitious with regard to a potential business investment that is nominal for start-up costs with the advantage of corporate support.

Participating in Fairs and Flea Markets:

Flea markets are everywhere and occur throughout the year. Bargain hunters come in huge numbers looking for the good value or the unusual. If your MLM products are related to jewelry, gifts, kitchenware or other household items, Flea Markets are very inexpensive venues that can offer exposure by word-of-mouth. While Fairs are mostly seasonal (typically summers), they are also filled with crowds looking for fun and enjoyable shopping. Perhaps with a joint marketing effort, MLM products can be offered as samples or giveaways, once again to create publicity and branding for MLM products or services.

Conducting Seminars with Professionals in a related field to your MLM Business:

If the MLM product or service is related to finance, real estate, insurance, nutrition or consumer services such as telecommunications or energy (a relatively new field), an informational seminar conducted with credentialed Professionals can deliver education and useful consumer knowledge. Once again it may be a cooperating Professional (with their own client base!) who is introduced to the MLM business who could be the prized Prospect who will join the company or at least use the products or pass the word to clients.

Joining Neighborhood Associations and participating in Community Events:

The local neighborhood or city district can be considered a version of a "Warm Market" if the MLM Practitioner is an active member of the community. Neighborhood associations develop bonds and friendships among members with a common interest which invariably involves community improvement. Community events, especially ethnic or interest/orientation-related are venues to approach people who may have normally not been approached by outside parties.

Utilizing creative "user-content" with high tech (free or cost-effective) Internet tools:

Internet social network marketing and high technology offer infinite varieties to create community, value, trust or just the plain power of numbers, speed and innovation. Consider starting your own blog or Podcast or creating an easily produced E-Book on your MLM opportunity, or producing a free YouTube presentation that serves to market your MLM business as well as hone your presentation skills!

21 Ps™

WORLD'S SUREST...FASTEST...SYSTEM FOR MONEY & SUCCESS...MLM CUSTOM GUIDEBOOK

SPECIAL TOOLS 4
CREATIVE MARKETING / "SUDU" (SUPER DUPLICATION) 30-DAY DRIVES

MORE ON "SUDU" (SUPER DUPLICATION) 30-DAY DRIVES

More details are discussed below on a few of the elements of "SUDU" Drives outlined in Chapter 14, Page 101. The overriding objective of the "SUDU" is to accomplish massive results in income and quality Recruits in a condensed period of time (30 Days) but that will be sustainable, buildable and long-lasting. A sense of urgency becomes a sense of "desperation" in that people are "desperate" for success and achievement that can come with an intensely motivated group of people. MLM activities are synergized, amplified and pushed to the limit by excitement, commitment and all-out effort.

COMMITMENT OF SPONSOR(S), TEAM AND ESPECIALLY THE "SUDU" REPRESENTATIVE

Nothing can be done without the complete commitment of the Representative's Sponsor. The Sponsor is experienced and skilled in all the activities that are concentrated in a "SUDU" Drive. The Sponsor must be available freely if not entirely for the 30 Days. The Sponsor must commit to pay for any costs (along with the Representative for all activities which may not be necessarily expensive). After all, the Sponsor is the ultimate beneficiary of the "SUDU" Representative's forthcoming massive success!

The Team must also contribute their time and effort in activities which have many indirect as well as direct and immediate benefits. Team members don't just learn skills, attitudes and techniques, they may also develop their own MLM businesses with the constant, continuous and multiple occasions to expose products and opportunity to their own customers and prospects. Excitement breeds excitement! Results domino to more results!

Obviously it is the "SUDU" Representative who must have absolute commitment to the 30 Days. There is no holding back. Every ounce of energy and every resource must be used. Any sacrifice or inconvenience or discomfort or anxiety will be soon replaced with relief, triumph and measurable results, as in income and Recruits! The adventures of the 30-Day SUDU will set the outlook and outcome of a bright future!

THE HEADQUARTERS OR HOME (OR OFFICE OR "SITE") FOR 30 DAYS:

The 30-Day main location of the "SUDU" drive is where "operations" are centralized as a Headquarters or a "War Room". This location is ideally a home where it is convenient for accommodations, meals, respite, groupings and regroupings, as well as the intense activities of Prospecting, Presentations, Gatherings, Appointments, Parties, Special Meetings, Strategy Sessions, Group Brainstorming, Product or Service Demonstrations, and Development Trainings. The "SUDU" Headquarters functions as the supply center, communications hub and a facility of physical and social activities. What would otherwise be just an ordinary place is a special site of bold and empowering actions.

While an office or even hotel meeting room can also serve as a "SUDU" central location, the advantages of a home setting prevails. In addition to familiarity, convenience and comfort for MLM participants, it is the very sacrifice of some privacy, convenience and comfort that demonstrates the "SUDU" Representative's commitment and seriousness to succeed. It will take the voluntary (perhaps begrudging) support of the "SUDU" Representative's family to allow for a house and residence to be taken over for 30 days by probably quite noisy and sometimes impolite MLM Practitioners who will be the main actors, players and in-and-out "guests" (and virtual "occupiers" for those who commit) of the great campaign. After 30 days, the house may become ordinary again but, its residents will never be the same!

SPECIAL TOOLS 4
CREATIVE MARKETING / "SUDU" (SUPER DUPLICATION) 30-DAY DRIVES

MORE ON "SUDU" (SUPER DUPLICATION) 30-DAY DRIVES -Continued

(MASSIVE) PROSPECTING

Being the most critical "technical" element of MLM success, Prospecting can be practiced, role-played, strategized, learned and fully conducted during the entire "SUDU" period. Representatives can rehearse scenarios and appointments that focus on listening, probing, understanding and presenting benefits to eventual Customers and Prospects. Scripts, listening postures and skills, attention-improvement and consultative selling can be drilled and re-drilled with the objective of external and inner mastery. 3-Way Calls can be prepared for and actually done with real Prospects. In a location where many Participants are doing the actual activities of Prospecting, the learning of winning styles (different among many) and the overcoming of mistakes and doubts are facilitated. It is scheduled that everyday actual Prospecting is done and it is expected that genuine Recruits for the business opportunity and actual Customers for the product or service will result!

PRESENTATIONS

Quantity and quality of Presentations are the explicit goals of a "SUDU". During a normal 30-Day period a new or even veteran Representative will typically attend 3 or 4 Formal Presentations. During a "SUDU", there could be 3 or 4 Effective Presentations (formal or otherwise) in a day! Imagine the rapid acquisition of skills and "experience" that can be amplified by a factor of 10 or even more! All in a compressed period of time with high probabilities for immediate positive and profitable outcomes!

Presentations can be conducted as the true social events that they are. A group of people gathered around the theme of products and an opportunity will "present" spontaneously. Picture the reaction of a Presentation guest or Prospect who sees and feels the energy of animated and enthusiastic people who are revolved around a dream for financial freedom and power. While Presentations should be scheduled for explicit times, an impromptu Presentation can occur when an important topic regarding products or the opportunity comes up. Presentations can become a social happening or vice versa as when a fun "party" can become indistinguishable from a demonstration of a product or opportunity benefit.

LEADERSHIP AND DEVELOPMENT TRAININGS

While the total 30-Days of the "SUDU" (Super Duplication) Drive is really a complete Leadership and Development Training, coaching, guidance and duplication take on entirely new meanings when everything can be done immediately and on the spot. There will inevitably very skilled and accomplished MLM Practitioners who will relish the chance to have an impact with their imparted wisdom and experience.

Imagine again the effects of immediacy and intensity of all the steps and actions of the MLM process come to life. Cause and effects can be demonstrated concretely and quickly. Productivity becomes natural in such a production-oriented setting as a 30-Day "SUDU" Drive. Perseverance becomes just a matter of trying again immediately because there is support and little time to dwell on "disappointments". Corrections can be made and applied fast to see if they hold. Practically speaking, there is little in the way of "giving up" or quitting. There is just too much momentum in a 30-Day "SUDU" Drive. The stage is set and the power of the moment and the tangibility of place make a powerful reality of success-expectation for all the players and real-life MLM Participants. What will come out are Leaders who beget more Leaders who accomplish their dreams!

21 Ps™

WORLD'S SUREST...FASTEST...SYSTEM FOR MONEY & SUCCESS...MLM CUSTOM GUIDEBOOK

SPECIAL TOOLS 4
CREATIVE MARKETING / "SUDU" (SUPER DUPLICATION) 30-DAY DRIVES

CONSIDERATIONS / ANALYSIS OF THE MLM TEAM
FOR A "SUDU" (SUPER DUPLICATION) 30-DAY DRIVE

SIZE OF MLM TEAM

There is no optimal size for an MLM Team undertaking a "SUDU" Drive. However the expected number of people should be comfortably accommodated by the physical space and resources available. 50 to 100 Representatives taking part in MLM activities in a "normal" size space of 1500 square feet of home (or 1000 square feet or so office space) over 30 days would be feasible with planning and management. It would be a "nice problem" to have if there were "too many" people being involved in Prospecting, Presentations, Demonstrations, Training and Signing-ups. Surely Team Sponsors can find a way to provide for more product-buying Customers and Prospects who want to join!

A logistical variation to the one home (or office) as the SUDU (Super Duplication) Headquarters is to divide the responsibilities of space and resources among a group (Top-Line or otherwise) Representatives. For example if there were 5 Representatives on the first level of the Sponsor, there could be 6 days of the 30 days allocated to each Representative; if there were only 3 "volunteers", then there could be a division of 10 days for each Representative to conduct their portion of the intense but highly productive SUDU Drive!

TEAM "BASELINE" and TEAM GOALS

An MLM Team must be defined in order to establish a baseline of group income and starting number of Representatives. For example, there could be a Sponsored Team of 5 Representatives with downlines of 3 or 4 Levels and a total of 45 downline Representatives comprising 50 Team Members overall. Over the course of the 30-Day SUDU Drive, downlines can get deeper and/or wider, with each leg developing according to a particular Representative's efforts, energy and motivation! The first level of the Sponsor (for example the 3 to 5 in total) can with the Sponsor share expenses and support the actual Representative (of any Level) who is providing the home or office.

With a baseline of, for example, 50 Team Members/Representatives, there will also be a baseline of group income produced by the 50 Representatives at the start of the 30 Day SUDU Drive. There will then be an avowed target goal for the Team. For instance if the 50 Representatives per month to date has produced $100,000 in income (commissions / bonuses / prizes), a target goal could be $200,000 of commissions / bonuses / prizes for the 30 day SUDU period. Additionally, there could be a target goal of 50 new Recruits!

THE 21 Ps SYSTEM and a 21 Ps CONSULTANT

An outside Consultant versed in the 21 Ps System would be an ideal Coordinator for a SUDU (Super Duplication) 30-Day Drive. No one on the Team would have to bear the sole responsibility of organizing, directing, scheduling and managing the 30-Day period and all its logistical and practical requirements.

A 21 Ps outside Consultant would focus on all the key aspects of the 21 Ps System, adapting the training according to the needs, levels of expertise and range of experiences among the MLM Participants. The various Programs in developing individual Representatives and the Team as a whole will be customized for the overall stated target goals which will be the explicit contractual task of the 21 Ps Consultant. For example, if the Team Goal is $100,000 in income growth and 50 new Recruits, the 21 Ps Consultant must deliver these results or according to the contract between the Consultant and the SUDU Team, certain negotiated fees will be paid or not! Please see Page 172 for further details regarding the services of the Author and his Associates.

21 Ps™

WORLD'S SUREST...FASTEST...SYSTEM FOR MONEY & SUCCESS...MLM CUSTOM GUIDEBOOK

DAILY CHECKLIST & NOTES FOR 30-DAY "SUDU" (SUPER DUPLICATION) DRIVE

Date: _____ (Day _____ of 30)

Prospecting: ☐ _____

Presentations: ☐ _____

Gatherings: ☐ _____

Appointments: ☐ _____

Parties: ☐ _____

Special Meetings: ☐ _____

Strategy Sessions: ☐ _____

Group Brainstorming: ☐ _____

Product or Service Demonstrations: ☐ _____

Development Trainings: ☐ _____

Sharing of Tools and Techniques: ☐ _____

Invitations of "Special Guests": ☐ _____

Recording of sessions on YouTube or other media: ☐ _____

Three-way Callings: ☐ _____

Massive Remote Conferencing: ☐ _____

Product "Sales": ☐ _____

Video Presentations: ☐ _____

Role-Playing and Simulations: ☐ _____

Neighborhood Specials: ☐ _____

Community Events: ☐ _____

Team Rallies: ☐ _____

Special Missions: ☐ _____

SPECIAL NOTES FOR DAY _____:

_____

_____

You can make 30 copies of this Page to cover entire SUDU. Attach the additional Pages to this Section for convenience/organization.

SPECIAL TOOL 5

REPRINT OF "THE ARTICLE" /

YOUR MLM COMPANY'S 3RD PARTY TOOLS

FOLLOWING IS A COPY OF THE PUBLISHED "YAHOO" ARTICLE THAT SERVES AS A POWERFUL PROSPECTING TOOL BY SURPRISINGLY DISARMING POTENTIAL RECRUITS WITH AN HONEST PORTRAYAL OF THE MLM INDUSTRY AND ITS PRODUCTS OR SERVICES AND OPPORTUNITY. THIS IS A "CONSUMER" ARTICLE IN THE BEST SENSE AS IT DIRECTLY ADDRESSES CUSTOMER AND PROSPECT CONCERNS BY BEING ABLE TO ANSWER THE LEGITIMATE CONCERNS OF THOSE WHO ARE INTERESTED AND THOSE WHO MAY BE UNINFORMED.

THE YAHOO CONSUMER ARTICLE IS REPRODUCED EXACTLY AS IT APPEARED IN EARLY IN 2011 (WITH AVAILABLE RESEARCH AT THAT TIME). STATISTICS AND FIGURES ON THE SIZE AND SCOPE OF THE MLM INDUSTRY ARE UPDATED IN THIS BOOK (SEE THIS BOOK'S INTRODUCTION AND SECTION 2 FOR SOME SPECIFIC MLM COMPANY INFO).

3RD PARTY TOOLS ARE EFFECTIVE FOR PROSPECTING AND GETTING CUSTOMERS. 3RD PARTY TOOLS SPECIFIC TO YOUR COMPANY AND IN GENERAL IN THE PROMOTION OF MLM AND BUSINESS (AND LIFE) SUCCESS MAKE THE CRITICAL PROCESS OF DUPLICATION POSSIBLE AND INEVITABLE IF THEY CAN REACH THE HANDS OF PROSPECTS-POTENTIAL BUSINESS-BUILDERS AND CUSTOMERS.

21 Ps™

WORLD'S SUREST...FASTEST...SYSTEM FOR MONEY & SUCCESS...MLM CUSTOM GUIDEBOOK

BLANK PAGE FOR

SPECIAL TOOLS 5

NOTES

21 Ps™

WORLD'S SUREST...FASTEST...SYSTEM FOR MONEY & SUCCESS...MLM CUSTOM GUIDEBOOK

SPECIAL TOOLS 5
REPRINT OF "THE ARTICLE" / YOUR MLM COMPANY'S 3rd PARTY TOOLS

YAHOO CONSUMER ARTICLE ON MLM (Page 1 of 2)

How to Review any Multi-Level Marketing Company, Keep Your Friends and Avoid Rip-Offs

A friend or family member keeps pestering you to look at "an amazing money-making business" of some great product or service that requires only a minimal investment. All you have to do is attend a "business opportunity meeting" at someone's house or at a nearby hotel. They finally confess or you find out that the opportunity is MLM (Multi-Level Marketing or Network Marketing) but you are assured that everything is legitimate. "No, this is not a pyramid scheme.....The products which you can get wholesale are revolutionary!.....You could make thousands of dollars fast, maybe tens of thousands, maybe hundreds of thousands, maybe millions..."

Sounds too good to be true? How do you respond appropriately and still keep your friendship or family relationship? How can you politely and assertively say no? Or if you are indeed curious about how you can possibly make extra income, how do you determine if the "opportunity" is real and even right for you and your circumstances? You need to perform the "5 Ps Test" that will make the person who is soliciting you prove at a minimum that their MLM Company is a legal and genuine business that might serve your needs. After the "5 Ps Test", you can say no tactfully or you can go forward, with further precautions and strategies to maximize your advantages, save money and avoid costly mistakes.

According to prolific writers/researchers in Multi-Level Marketing, Rod Nichols and Sue Seward (Entrepreneur Magazine, January 2007 & Home Business Magazine, December 2010), the network marketing industry now has over 3,000 companies, 50 million representatives and sales of over $100 billion worldwide with a 91% growth in the last 10 years. With successful and long-established MLM companies such as Amway, Mary Kay, Avon and Tupperware network marketing has become a proven business and marketing/distribution model.

Despite problems from public misunderstanding and a few fraudulent companies, today's networking companies feature legitimate products and services that offer income opportunities for the right person who decides to seriously and systematically pursue a business through hard work, patience and perseverance. Millions of individuals around the world have achieved success in otherwise limited economic conditions, especially women.

Network Marketing is especially suited to the Internet age with the ability for a representative to market products anywhere and anytime with the company's representative-customized website. Requiring no technical skills or special knowledge, just about anyone can join a company with a relatively small investment (although new representatives must be aware of the pressure or risk of buying too many products initially).

Even if network marketing is easy to enter and start, the business is not for everyone. Problems in the past (and present) have arisen because of personal misconceptions as well as company deficiencies. Sometimes products, the company and the concept of network marketing are overhyped resulting in unreal expectations, disappointment and failures. Network marketing success is slow in building (like most careers) taking up to 5 years to be fully profitable. While a company may have thousands or tens of thousands (as in the larger MLM companies) of productive practitioners, there is a high turnover rate of those joining and quitting the business.

Lack of success in network marketing stems from lack of work and effort by individual representatives and is worsened by a company's lack of training and support. Furthermore, new representatives are first very excited by compensation plans that are eventually difficult to attain or are too complex to understand. When a company's compensation is very lucrative for the big producers at the expense of the average or new representative, motivation to continue and work at the business wanes and leads to failure.

Still, network marketing is booming and finding the right company with the right products and/or services may be the answer in the tough economic times in industrialized countries and may still be one of the few opportunities for women in the developing world. Laid-off workers are familiar with network marketing as a home-based business that can supplement or replace lost income. Many MLM companies are household names with their own famous brands. Even the billionaire Warren Buffet has been involved with MLM Companies (his Berkshire Hathaway owns the Pampered Chef, and once owned World Book and Kirby Vacuum).

21 Ps™

WORLD'S SUREST...FASTEST...SYSTEM FOR MONEY & SUCCESS...MLM CUSTOM GUIDEBOOK

SPECIAL TOOLS 5
REPRINT OF "THE ARTICLE" / YOUR MLM COMPANY'S 3ʳᵈ PARTY TOOLS

YAHOO CONSUMER ARTICLE ON MLM (Page 2 of 2)

"THE 5 Ps TEST": Questions and Issues for the Person Who Is Soliciting or Recruiting You for MLM to Answer

PROPOSITION
What is your company all about in terms of product, mission and history (in summary), including valid testimonials and honest reviews of the company? What makes your company unique or special?

PRODUCT or SERVICE
What are your company's specific products or services with its unique or special benefits, values or "ingredients"? Where are your products made and who makes them? Show honest reviews of your products or services, including any negative ones and the sources (objective) of the reviews. Even competing products should be compared.

PEOPLE
Who are the members and leaders up and down in your organization and what are their past backgrounds in business, the community and also personally. Leaders must have solid reputations, without criminal or shady histories. How do you (the person recruiting or soliciting) fit in the company? Share personal stories that tell of your genuine reasons for joining the company, including any hardships or challenges or real accomplishments.

PRICING (and Competition)
What are prices of products (and services) and what are special promotions and pricing advantages for members and "leaders"? Present Catalogs and Full Price Lists. Again compare prices to competition and justify any higher costs.

PAY
What are your company's "compensation" plans? Summarize programs and include honest and true figures for specific members including your own profits or gains. Tell about outstanding performers and earners, including those with "normal" income. People want honesty! Some are just looking for part-time opportunities or decent money!

If your recruiter and the MLM company pass the above test with excellent marks, consider joining but only after attending at least 3 -5 meetings, depending on your time availability. Let the company work hard in "recruiting" you. If you intend to sign up, wait for the inevitable product promotions for joining, including product discounts and reduced sign up fees. Try all the products you are interested in and ask for free samples or drastically reduced prices. If you do sign up, do NOT agree to any "Auto-Ship" (automatic monthly minimum orders that you have to pay for!) unless you truly have customers/buyers ready to use and pay for the products. Resist the pressures of being placed as a "Manager" or Director" or similar "high commission" position achieved only through buying large volumes of products, even at a "preferred" discount. You may never recoup your investment. "Take your time and save your dime!"

Do not be blindly impressed by those who seem to be very successful in a particular MLM Company. Most "top achievers" will probably still keep their "day jobs" which would indicate that their "off-the chart" income may be inflated or short-lived. Joining an MLM Company means going to work and growing a business (remember the 5-year build-up) and being good in all the usual skills required for success: persistence, knowledge and belief in your product or service, and long hours performing sales, accounting and strategizing, not to mention all those meetings at a hotel or perhaps now your own house where you are trying to attract new customers and recruits who all should make you complete the "5 Ps Test".

Finally just beware of MLM companies who seem to talk more about recruiting than the actual product or service which is the foundation of the entire network marketing business. Just say, "Sorry, not for me at this time." Analyze the MLM opportunity presented and do yourself and your friend or family member a favor. There are many choices for excellent MLM Companies with products and services that may be right for you to use and sell. Best of luck!

You can show a recruiter this article as a response to a solicitation or if you are presently involved in an MLM Company, use it as your own tool to get potential customers.

21 Ps™

WORLD'S SUREST...FASTEST...SYSTEM FOR MONEY & SUCCESS...MLM CUSTOM GUIDEBOOK

SPECIAL TOOLS 5
REPRINT OF "THE ARTICLE" / YOUR MLM COMPANY'S 3rd PARTY TOOLS

LIST BELOW THE SPECIFIC 3RD PARTY TOOLS OF YOUR MLM COMPANY:
(Specific CDs, Books, Brochures, Marketing and Promotional Materials, and Product Samples)
-Include price, quantities and availability, and sources or access-

_____

_____

_____

_____

_____

_____

_____

_____

_____

_____

_____

_____

_____

_____

_____

_____

_____

_____

21 Ps™
WORLD'S SUREST...FASTEST...SYSTEM FOR MONEY & SUCCESS...MLM CUSTOM GUIDEBOOK

BLANK PAGE

BONUS:

CUSTOMIZABLE

CALENDAR

OF DAILY & <u>HOURLY</u> ACTIVITIES

FOR 6 MONTHS

-START AT ANY MONTH/YEAR-

21 Ps™

WORLD'S SUREST...FASTEST...SYSTEM FOR MONEY & SUCCESS...MLM CUSTOM GUIDEBOOK

CALENDAR
DAILY & HOURLY ACTIVITIES FOR 6 MONTHS (START AT ANY MONTH)

YEAR: _____ : WEEK 1 of MONTH ____ : 1st Half of Week

PRIORITIES/EVENTS/APPOINTMENTS OF THE WEEK:	Monday Today's Main Focus or Priority	Tuesday Today's Main Focus or Priority	Wednesday Today's Main Focus or Priority
_____			
_____			
_____			
_____	MORNING:	MORNING:	MORNING:
- - - - - - - - - - - - - - - - - - - -			
Small Goal 1:			
_____			
Success(es):			
_____	9am	9am	9am
_____	10am	10am	10am
- - - - - - - - - - - - - - - - - - - -	11am	11am	11am
Small Goal 2:	12noon	12noon	12noon
_____	1pm	1pm	1pm
Success(es):	2pm	2pm	2pm
_____	3pm	3pm	3pm
_____	4pm	4pm	4pm
- - - - - - - - - - - - - - - - - - - -	5pm	5pm	5pm
BIG Goal 1:	6pm	6pm	6pm
Deadline: _____	7pm	7pm	7pm
Success(es):	8pm	8pm	8pm
_____	EVENING/NIGHT:	EVENING/NIGHT:	EVENING/NIGHT:
_____			

Note: Small Goals must support Big Goals which have deadlines. Connect these Big Goals to the Monthly & Yearly Time-lines

- -

WEEKLY TRAINING
List at least 1 "P" Focused on:

21 Ps™

WORLD'S SUREST...FASTEST...SYSTEM FOR MONEY & SUCCESS...MLM CUSTOM GUIDEBOOK

CALENDAR
DAILY & HOURLY ACTIVITIES FOR 6 MONTHS (START AT ANY MONTH)

YEAR: _____ : WEEK 1 of MONTH _____ : 2nd Half of Week

Thursday Today's Main Focus or Priority	Friday Today's Main Focus or Priority	Saturday Today's Main Focus or Priority	Sunday Today's Main Focus or Priority	NOTES:
_____ _____	_____ _____	_____ _____	_____ _____	
MORNING:	MORNING:	MORNING:	MORNING:	
_____ _____ _____ _____	_____ _____ _____ _____	_____ _____ _____ _____	_____ _____ _____ _____	
9am	9am	9am	9am	
10am	10am	10am	10am	
11am	11am	11am	11am	
12noon	12noon	12noon	12noon	
1pm	1pm	1pm	1pm	
2pm	2pm	2pm	2pm	
3pm	3pm	3pm	3pm	
4pm	4pm	4pm	4pm	
5pm	5pm	5pm	5pm	
6pm	6pm	6pm	6pm	
7pm	7pm	7pm	7pm	
8pm	8pm	8pm	8pm	
EVENING/NIGHT:	EVENING/NIGHT:	EVENING/NIGHT:	EVENING/NIGHT:	
_____ _____ _____ _____	_____ _____ _____ _____	_____ _____ _____ _____	_____ _____ _____ _____	

21 Ps™

WORLD'S SUREST...FASTEST...SYSTEM FOR MONEY & SUCCESS...MLM CUSTOM GUIDEBOOK

CALENDAR
DAILY & HOURLY ACTIVITIES FOR 6 MONTHS (START AT ANY MONTH)

YEAR: _____ : WEEK 2 of MONTH _____ : 1st Half of Week

PRIORITIES/EVENTS/APPOINTMENTS OF THE WEEK:	Monday Today's Main Focus or Priority	Tuesday Today's Main Focus or Priority	Wednesday Today's Main Focus or Priority
_____ _____ _____ _____ ---------------------------------- Small Goal 1: _____ Success(es): _____ _____ ---------------------------------- Small Goal 2: _____ Success(es): _____ _____ ---------------------------------- BIG Goal 1: **Deadline**: _____ Success(es): _____ _____ Note: Small Goals must support Big Goals which have deadlines. Connect these Big Goals to the Monthly & Yearly Time-lines ---------------------------------- WEEKLY TRAINING List at least 1 "P" Focused on: _____	_____ _____ MORNING: _____ _____ _____ _____ 9am 10am 11am 12noon 1pm 2pm 3pm 4pm 5pm 6pm 7pm 8pm EVENING/NIGHT: _____ _____ _____ _____ _____	_____ _____ MORNING: _____ _____ _____ _____ 9am 10am 11am 12noon 1pm 2pm 3pm 4pm 5pm 6pm 7pm 8pm EVENING/NIGHT: _____ _____ _____ _____ _____	_____ _____ MORNING: _____ _____ _____ _____ 9am 10am 11am 12noon 1pm 2pm 3pm 4pm 5pm 6pm 7pm 8pm EVENING/NIGHT: _____ _____ _____ _____ _____

21 Ps™

WORLD'S SUREST...FASTEST...SYSTEM FOR MONEY & SUCCESS...MLM CUSTOM GUIDEBOOK

CALENDAR
DAILY & HOURLY ACTIVITIES FOR 6 MONTHS (START AT ANY MONTH)

YEAR: _____ : WEEK 2 of MONTH _____ : 2nd Half of Week

Thursday Today's Main Focus or Priority	Friday Today's Main Focus or Priority	Saturday Today's Main Focus or Priority	Sunday Today's Main Focus or Priority	NOTES:
_____ _____ MORNING:	_____ _____ MORNING:	_____ _____ MORNING:	_____ _____ MORNING:	
9am	9am	9am	9am	
10am	10am	10am	10am	
11am	11am	11am	11am	
12noon	12noon	12noon	12noon	
1pm	1pm	1pm	1pm	
2pm	2pm	2pm	2pm	
3pm	3pm	3pm	3pm	
4pm	4pm	4pm	4pm	
5pm	5pm	5pm	5pm	
6pm	6pm	6pm	6pm	
7pm	7pm	7pm	7pm	
8pm	8pm	8pm	8pm	
EVENING/NIGHT:	EVENING/NIGHT:	EVENING/NIGHT:	EVENING/NIGHT:	

21 Ps™

WORLD'S SUREST...FASTEST...SYSTEM FOR MONEY & SUCCESS...MLM CUSTOM GUIDEBOOK

CALENDAR
DAILY & HOURLY ACTIVITIES FOR 6 MONTHS (START AT ANY MONTH)

YEAR: _____ : WEEK 3 of MONTH _____ : 1st Half of Week

PRIORITIES/EVENTS/APPOINTMENTS OF THE WEEK:	Monday Today's Main Focus or Priority	Tuesday Today's Main Focus or Priority	Wednesday Today's Main Focus or Priority
_____	_____	_____	_____
_____	_____	_____	_____
_____	MORNING:	MORNING:	MORNING:
_____	_____	_____	_____
- - - - - - - - - - - - - - - - - -	_____	_____	_____
Small Goal 1:	_____	_____	_____
Success(es):	_____	_____	_____
_____	9am	9am	9am
_____	10am	10am	10am
- - - - - - - - - - - - - - - - - -	11am	11am	11am
Small Goal 2:	12noon	12noon	12noon
_____	1pm	1pm	1pm
Success(es):	2pm	2pm	2pm
_____	3pm	3pm	3pm
_____	4pm	4pm	4pm
- - - - - - - - - - - - - - - - - -	5pm	5pm	5pm
BIG Goal 1:	6pm	6pm	6pm
Deadline: _____	7pm	7pm	7pm
Success(es):	8pm	8pm	8pm
_____	EVENING/NIGHT:	EVENING/NIGHT:	EVENING/NIGHT:
Note: Small Goals must support Big Goals which have deadlines. Connect these Big Goals to the Monthly & Yearly Time-lines	_____	_____	_____
- - - - - - - - - - - - - - - - - -	_____	_____	_____
WEEKLY TRAINING List at least 1 "P" Focused on:	_____	_____	_____
_____	_____	_____	_____

21 Ps™

WORLD'S SUREST...FASTEST...SYSTEM FOR MONEY & SUCCESS...MLM CUSTOM GUIDEBOOK

CALENDAR
DAILY & HOURLY ACTIVITIES FOR 6 MONTHS (START AT ANY MONTH)

YEAR: _____ : WEEK 3 of MONTH ____ : 2nd Half of Week

Thursday Today's Main Focus or Priority	Friday Today's Main Focus or Priority	Saturday Today's Main Focus or Priority	Sunday Today's Main Focus or Priority	NOTES:
_____ _____ MORNING:	_____ _____ MORNING:	_____ _____ MORNING:	_____ _____ MORNING:	
9am	9am	9am	9am	
10am	10am	10am	10am	
11am	11am	11am	11am	
12noon	12noon	12noon	12noon	
1pm	1pm	1pm	1pm	
2pm	2pm	2pm	2pm	
3pm	3pm	3pm	3pm	
4pm	4pm	4pm	4pm	
5pm	5pm	5pm	5pm	
6pm	6pm	6pm	6pm	
7pm	7pm	7pm	7pm	
8pm	8pm	8pm	8pm	
EVENING/NIGHT:	EVENING/NIGHT:	EVENING/NIGHT:	EVENING/NIGHT:	

21 Ps™

WORLD'S SUREST...FASTEST...SYSTEM FOR MONEY & SUCCESS...MLM CUSTOM GUIDEBOOK

CALENDAR
DAILY & HOURLY ACTIVITIES FOR 6 MONTHS (START AT ANY MONTH)

YEAR: _____ : WEEK 4 of MONTH _____ : 1st Half of Week

PRIORITIES/EVENTS/APPOINTMENTS OF THE WEEK:	Monday Today's Main Focus or Priority	Tuesday Today's Main Focus or Priority	Wednesday Today's Main Focus or Priority
_____			
_____			
_____	MORNING:	MORNING:	MORNING:
_____			

Small Goal 1:			
Success(es):	9am	9am	9am
_____	10am	10am	10am
_____	11am	11am	11am
---------------------------	12noon	12noon	12noon
Small Goal 2:	1pm	1pm	1pm
_____	2pm	2pm	2pm
Success(es):	3pm	3pm	3pm
_____	4pm	4pm	4pm
_____	5pm	5pm	5pm
---------------------------	6pm	6pm	6pm
BIG Goal 1:	7pm	7pm	7pm
Deadline: _____	8pm	8pm	8pm
Success(es):			
_____	EVENING/NIGHT:	EVENING/NIGHT:	EVENING/NIGHT:
_____			
Note: Small Goals must support Big Goals which have deadlines. Connect these Big Goals to the Monthly & Yearly Time-lines			

WEEKLY TRAINING List at least 1 "P" Focused on:			
_____			

21 Ps™

WORLD'S SUREST...FASTEST...SYSTEM FOR MONEY & SUCCESS...MLM CUSTOM GUIDEBOOK

CALENDAR
DAILY & HOURLY ACTIVITIES FOR 6 MONTHS (START AT ANY MONTH)

YEAR: _____ : WEEK 4 of MONTH _____ : 2nd Half of Week

Thursday Today's Main Focus or Priority	Friday Today's Main Focus or Priority	Saturday Today's Main Focus or Priority	Sunday Today's Main Focus or Priority	NOTES:
_____ _____	_____ _____	_____ _____	_____ _____	
MORNING:	MORNING:	MORNING:	MORNING:	
9am	9am	9am	9am	
10am	10am	10am	10am	
11am	11am	11am	11am	
12noon	12noon	12noon	12noon	
1pm	1pm	1pm	1pm	
2pm	2pm	2pm	2pm	
3pm	3pm	3pm	3pm	
4pm	4pm	4pm	4pm	
5pm	5pm	5pm	5pm	
6pm	6pm	6pm	6pm	
7pm	7pm	7pm	7pm	
8pm	8pm	8pm	8pm	
EVENING/NIGHT:	EVENING/NIGHT:	EVENING/NIGHT:	EVENING/NIGHT:	

21 Ps™

WORLD'S SUREST...FASTEST...SYSTEM FOR MONEY & SUCCESS...MLM CUSTOM GUIDEBOOK

CALENDAR
DAILY & HOURLY ACTIVITIES FOR 6 MONTHS (START AT ANY MONTH)

YEAR: _____ : WEEK 5 of MONTH _____ : 1ˢᵗ Half of Week

PRIORITIES/EVENTS/APPOINTMENTS OF THE WEEK:	Monday Today's Main Focus or Priority	Tuesday Today's Main Focus or Priority	Wednesday Today's Main Focus or Priority
_____	_____	_____	_____
_____	_____	_____	_____
_____	MORNING:	MORNING:	MORNING:
_____	_____	_____	_____
------------------------------------	_____	_____	_____
Small Goal 1:	_____	_____	_____
_____	_____	_____	_____
Success(es):	9am	9am	9am
_____	10am	10am	10am
_____	11am	11am	11am
------------------------------------	12noon	12noon	12noon
Small Goal 2:	1pm	1pm	1pm
_____	2pm	2pm	2pm
Success(es):	3pm	3pm	3pm
_____	4pm	4pm	4pm
_____	5pm	5pm	5pm
------------------------------------	6pm	6pm	6pm
BIG Goal 1:	7pm	7pm	7pm
Deadline: _____	8pm	8pm	8pm
Success(es):			
_____	EVENING/NIGHT:	EVENING/NIGHT:	EVENING/NIGHT:
_____	_____	_____	_____
Note: Small Goals must support Big Goals which have deadlines. Connect these Big Goals to the Monthly & Yearly Time-lines	_____	_____	_____
------------------------------------	_____	_____	_____
WEEKLY TRAINING List at least 1 "P" Focused on:	_____	_____	_____
_____	_____	_____	_____

21 Ps™

WORLD'S SUREST...FASTEST...SYSTEM FOR MONEY & SUCCESS...MLM CUSTOM GUIDEBOOK

CALENDAR
DAILY & HOURLY ACTIVITIES FOR 6 MONTHS (START AT ANY MONTH)

YEAR: _____ : WEEK 5 of MONTH _____ : 2nd Half of Week

Thursday Today's Main Focus or Priority	Friday Today's Main Focus or Priority	Saturday Today's Main Focus or Priority	Sunday Today's Main Focus or Priority	NOTES:
MORNING:	MORNING:	MORNING:	MORNING:	
9am	9am	9am	9am	
10am	10am	10am	10am	
11am	11am	11am	11am	
12noon	12noon	12noon	12noon	
1pm	1pm	1pm	1pm	
2pm	2pm	2pm	2pm	
3pm	3pm	3pm	3pm	
4pm	4pm	4pm	4pm	
5pm	5pm	5pm	5pm	
6pm	6pm	6pm	6pm	
7pm	7pm	7pm	7pm	
8pm	8pm	8pm	8pm	
EVENING/NIGHT:	EVENING/NIGHT:	EVENING/NIGHT:	EVENING/NIGHT:	

21 Ps™

WORLD'S SUREST...FASTEST...SYSTEM FOR MONEY & SUCCESS...MLM CUSTOM GUIDEBOOK

CALENDAR
DAILY & HOURLY ACTIVITIES FOR 6 MONTHS (START AT ANY MONTH)

YEAR: _____ : WEEK 1 of MONTH ____ : 1st Half of Week

PRIORITIES/EVENTS/APPOINTMENTS OF THE WEEK:	Monday Today's Main Focus or Priority	Tuesday Today's Main Focus or Priority	Wednesday Today's Main Focus or Priority
_____			
_____			
_____	MORNING:	MORNING:	MORNING:
_____			

Small Goal 1:			
Success(es):			
_____	9am	9am	9am
_____	10am	10am	10am
----------------------------	11am	11am	11am
Small Goal 2:	12noon	12noon	12noon
_____	1pm	1pm	1pm
Success(es):	2pm	2pm	2pm
_____	3pm	3pm	3pm
_____	4pm	4pm	4pm
----------------------------	5pm	5pm	5pm
BIG Goal 1:	6pm	6pm	6pm
Deadline: _____	7pm	7pm	7pm
Success(es):	8pm	8pm	8pm
_____	EVENING/NIGHT:	EVENING/NIGHT:	EVENING/NIGHT:
_____			
Note: Small Goals must support Big Goals which have deadlines. Connect these Big Goals to the Monthly & Yearly Time-lines			

WEEKLY TRAINING List at least 1 "P" Focused on:			
_____			

21 Ps™

WORLD'S SUREST...FASTEST...SYSTEM FOR MONEY & SUCCESS...MLM CUSTOM GUIDEBOOK

CALENDAR
DAILY & HOURLY ACTIVITIES FOR 6 MONTHS (START AT ANY MONTH)

YEAR: _____ : WEEK 1 of MONTH _____ : 2nd Half of Week

Thursday Today's Main Focus or Priority	Friday Today's Main Focus or Priority	Saturday Today's Main Focus or Priority	Sunday Today's Main Focus or Priority	NOTES:
_____ _____	_____ _____	_____ _____	_____ _____	
MORNING:	MORNING:	MORNING:	MORNING:	
9am	9am	9am	9am	
10am	10am	10am	10am	
11am	11am	11am	11am	
12noon	12noon	12noon	12noon	
1pm	1pm	1pm	1pm	
2pm	2pm	2pm	2pm	
3pm	3pm	3pm	3pm	
4pm	4pm	4pm	4pm	
5pm	5pm	5pm	5pm	
6pm	6pm	6pm	6pm	
7pm	7pm	7pm	7pm	
8pm	8pm	8pm	8pm	
EVENING/NIGHT:	EVENING/NIGHT:	EVENING/NIGHT:	EVENING/NIGHT:	

21 Ps™

WORLD'S SUREST...FASTEST...SYSTEM FOR MONEY & SUCCESS...MLM CUSTOM GUIDEBOOK

CALENDAR
DAILY & HOURLY ACTIVITIES FOR 6 MONTHS (START AT ANY MONTH)

YEAR: _____ : WEEK 2 of MONTH _____ : 1st Half of Week

PRIORITIES/EVENTS/APPOINTMENTS OF THE WEEK:	Monday Today's Main Focus or Priority	Tuesday Today's Main Focus or Priority	Wednesday Today's Main Focus or Priority
_____	_____	_____	_____
_____	_____	_____	_____
_____	MORNING:	MORNING:	MORNING:
_____			
- - - - - - - - - - - - - - - - - -			
Small Goal 1:			
Success(es):			
_____	9am	9am	9am
	10am	10am	10am
- - - - - - - - - - - - - - - - - -	11am	11am	11am
Small Goal 2:	12noon	12noon	12noon
	1pm	1pm	1pm
Success(es):	2pm	2pm	2pm
	3pm	3pm	3pm
_____	4pm	4pm	4pm
- - - - - - - - - - - - - - - - - -	5pm	5pm	5pm
BIG Goal 1:	6pm	6pm	6pm
Deadline: _____	7pm	7pm	7pm
Success(es):	8pm	8pm	8pm
_____	EVENING/NIGHT:	EVENING/NIGHT:	EVENING/NIGHT:
Note: Small Goals must support Big Goals which have deadlines. Connect these Big Goals to the Monthly & Yearly Time-lines			
- - - - - - - - - - - - - - - - - -			
WEEKLY TRAINING List at least 1 "P" Focused on:			
_____			

21 Ps™

WORLD'S SUREST...FASTEST...SYSTEM FOR MONEY & SUCCESS...MLM CUSTOM GUIDEBOOK

CALENDAR
DAILY & HOURLY ACTIVITIES FOR 6 MONTHS (START AT ANY MONTH)

YEAR: _____ : WEEK 2 of MONTH _____ : 2nd Half of Week

Thursday Today's Main Focus or Priority	Friday Today's Main Focus or Priority	Saturday Today's Main Focus or Priority	Sunday Today's Main Focus or Priority	NOTES:
_____ _____ MORNING:	_____ _____ MORNING:	_____ _____ MORNING:	_____ _____ MORNING:	
9am	9am	9am	9am	
10am	10am	10am	10am	
11am	11am	11am	11am	
12noon	12noon	12noon	12noon	
1pm	1pm	1pm	1pm	
2pm	2pm	2pm	2pm	
3pm	3pm	3pm	3pm	
4pm	4pm	4pm	4pm	
5pm	5pm	5pm	5pm	
6pm	6pm	6pm	6pm	
7pm	7pm	7pm	7pm	
8pm	8pm	8pm	8pm	
EVENING/NIGHT:	EVENING/NIGHT:	EVENING/NIGHT:	EVENING/NIGHT:	

21 Ps™

WORLD'S SUREST...FASTEST...SYSTEM FOR MONEY & SUCCESS...MLM CUSTOM GUIDEBOOK

CALENDAR
DAILY & HOURLY ACTIVITIES FOR 6 MONTHS (START AT ANY MONTH)

YEAR: _____ : WEEK 3 of MONTH _____ : 1st Half of Week

PRIORITIES/EVENTS/APPOINTMENTS OF THE WEEK:	Monday Today's Main Focus or Priority	Tuesday Today's Main Focus or Priority	Wednesday Today's Main Focus or Priority
_____			
_____			
_____	MORNING:	MORNING:	MORNING:
_____			

Small Goal 1:			
_____			
Success(es):	9am	9am	9am
_____	10am	10am	10am
------------------------------	11am	11am	11am
Small Goal 2:	12noon	12noon	12noon
_____	1pm	1pm	1pm
Success(es):	2pm	2pm	2pm
_____	3pm	3pm	3pm
_____	4pm	4pm	4pm
------------------------------	5pm	5pm	5pm
BIG Goal 1:	6pm	6pm	6pm
Deadline: _____	7pm	7pm	7pm
Success(es):	8pm	8pm	8pm
_____	EVENING/NIGHT:	EVENING/NIGHT:	EVENING/NIGHT:
Note: Small Goals must support Big Goals which have deadlines. Connect these Big Goals to the Monthly & Yearly Time-lines			

WEEKLY TRAINING List at least 1 "P" Focused on:			
_____			

21 Ps™

WORLD'S SUREST...FASTEST...SYSTEM FOR MONEY & SUCCESS...MLM CUSTOM GUIDEBOOK

CALENDAR
DAILY & HOURLY ACTIVITIES FOR 6 MONTHS (START AT ANY MONTH)

YEAR: _____ : WEEK 3 of MONTH _____ : 2nd Half of Week

Thursday Today's Main Focus or Priority	Friday Today's Main Focus or Priority	Saturday Today's Main Focus or Priority	Sunday Today's Main Focus or Priority	NOTES:
_____	_____	_____	_____	
_____	_____	_____	_____	
MORNING:	MORNING:	MORNING:	MORNING:	
_____	_____	_____	_____	
_____	_____	_____	_____	
_____	_____	_____	_____	
_____	_____	_____	_____	
9am	9am	9am	9am	
10am	10am	10am	10am	
11am	11am	11am	11am	
12noon	12noon	12noon	12noon	
1pm	1pm	1pm	1pm	
2pm	2pm	2pm	2pm	
3pm	3pm	3pm	3pm	
4pm	4pm	4pm	4pm	
5pm	5pm	5pm	5pm	
6pm	6pm	6pm	6pm	
7pm	7pm	7pm	7pm	
8pm	8pm	8pm	8pm	
EVENING/NIGHT:	EVENING/NIGHT:	EVENING/NIGHT:	EVENING/NIGHT:	
_____	_____	_____	_____	
_____	_____	_____	_____	
_____	_____	_____	_____	
_____	_____	_____	_____	
_____	_____	_____	_____	

21 Ps™

WORLD'S SUREST...FASTEST...SYSTEM FOR MONEY & SUCCESS...MLM CUSTOM GUIDEBOOK

CALENDAR
DAILY & HOURLY ACTIVITIES FOR 6 MONTHS (START AT ANY MONTH)

YEAR: _____ : WEEK 4 of MONTH _____ : 1st Half of Week

PRIORITIES/EVENTS/APPOINTMENTS OF THE WEEK:	Monday Today's Main Focus or Priority	Tuesday Today's Main Focus or Priority	Wednesday Today's Main Focus or Priority
_____	_____	_____	_____
_____	_____	_____	_____
_____	MORNING:	MORNING:	MORNING:
_____	_____	_____	_____
---	_____	_____	_____
Small Goal 1:	_____	_____	_____
_____	_____	_____	_____
Success(es):	9am	9am	9am
_____	10am	10am	10am
---	11am	11am	11am
Small Goal 2:	12noon	12noon	12noon
_____	1pm	1pm	1pm
Success(es):	2pm	2pm	2pm
_____	3pm	3pm	3pm
---	4pm	4pm	4pm
BIG Goal 1:	5pm	5pm	5pm
Deadline: _____	6pm	6pm	6pm
Success(es):	7pm	7pm	7pm
_____	8pm	8pm	8pm
_____	EVENING/NIGHT:	EVENING/NIGHT:	EVENING/NIGHT:
Note: Small Goals must support Big Goals which have deadlines. Connect these Big Goals to the Monthly & Yearly Time-lines	_____	_____	_____
---	_____	_____	_____
WEEKLY TRAINING List at least 1 "P" Focused on:	_____	_____	_____
_____	_____	_____	_____

21 Ps™

WORLD'S SUREST...FASTEST...SYSTEM FOR MONEY & SUCCESS...MLM CUSTOM GUIDEBOOK

CALENDAR
DAILY & HOURLY ACTIVITIES FOR 6 MONTHS (START AT ANY MONTH)

YEAR: _____ : WEEK 4 of MONTH _____ : 2nd Half of Week

Thursday Today's Main Focus or Priority	Friday Today's Main Focus or Priority	Saturday Today's Main Focus or Priority	Sunday Today's Main Focus or Priority	NOTES:
_____ _____	_____ _____	_____ _____	_____ _____	
MORNING:	MORNING:	MORNING:	MORNING:	
9am	9am	9am	9am	
10am	10am	10am	10am	
11am	11am	11am	11am	
12noon	12noon	12noon	12noon	
1pm	1pm	1pm	1pm	
2pm	2pm	2pm	2pm	
3pm	3pm	3pm	3pm	
4pm	4pm	4pm	4pm	
5pm	5pm	5pm	5pm	
6pm	6pm	6pm	6pm	
7pm	7pm	7pm	7pm	
8pm	8pm	8pm	8pm	
EVENING/NIGHT:	EVENING/NIGHT:	EVENING/NIGHT:	EVENING/NIGHT:	

21 Ps™

WORLD'S SUREST...FASTEST...SYSTEM FOR MONEY & SUCCESS...MLM CUSTOM GUIDEBOOK

CALENDAR
DAILY & HOURLY ACTIVITIES FOR 6 MONTHS (START AT ANY MONTH)

YEAR: _____ : WEEK 5 of MONTH _____ : 1st Half of Week

PRIORITIES/EVENTS/APPOINTMENTS OF THE WEEK:	Monday Today's Main Focus or Priority	Tuesday Today's Main Focus or Priority	Wednesday Today's Main Focus or Priority
_____	_____	_____	_____
_____	_____	_____	_____
_____	MORNING:	MORNING:	MORNING:
_____	_____	_____	_____
Small Goal 1:	_____	_____	_____
Success(es):	_____	_____	_____
_____	9am	9am	9am
_____	10am	10am	10am
Small Goal 2:	11am	11am	11am
Success(es):	12noon	12noon	12noon
_____	1pm	1pm	1pm
_____	2pm	2pm	2pm
_____	3pm	3pm	3pm
BIG Goal 1:	4pm	4pm	4pm
	5pm	5pm	5pm
Deadline: _____	6pm	6pm	6pm
Success(es):	7pm	7pm	7pm
_____	8pm	8pm	8pm
_____	EVENING/NIGHT:	EVENING/NIGHT:	EVENING/NIGHT:
Note: Small Goals must support Big Goals which have deadlines. Connect these Big Goals to the Monthly & Yearly Time-lines	_____	_____	_____
WEEKLY TRAINING List at least 1 "P" Focused on:	_____	_____	_____
_____	_____	_____	_____

21 Ps™

WORLD'S SUREST...FASTEST...SYSTEM FOR MONEY & SUCCESS...MLM CUSTOM GUIDEBOOK

CALENDAR
DAILY & HOURLY ACTIVITIES FOR 6 MONTHS (START AT ANY MONTH)

YEAR: _____ : WEEK 5 of MONTH _____ : 2nd Half of Week

Thursday Today's Main Focus or Priority	Friday Today's Main Focus or Priority	Saturday Today's Main Focus or Priority	Sunday Today's Main Focus or Priority	NOTES:
_____	_____	_____	_____	
_____	_____	_____	_____	
MORNING:	MORNING:	MORNING:	MORNING:	
_____	_____	_____	_____	
_____	_____	_____	_____	
_____	_____	_____	_____	
_____	_____	_____	_____	
9am	9am	9am	9am	
10am	10am	10am	10am	
11am	11am	11am	11am	
12noon	12noon	12noon	12noon	
1pm	1pm	1pm	1pm	
2pm	2pm	2pm	2pm	
3pm	3pm	3pm	3pm	
4pm	4pm	4pm	4pm	
5pm	5pm	5pm	5pm	
6pm	6pm	6pm	6pm	
7pm	7pm	7pm	7pm	
8pm	8pm	8pm	8pm	
EVENING/NIGHT:	EVENING/NIGHT:	EVENING/NIGHT:	EVENING/NIGHT:	
_____	_____	_____	_____	
_____	_____	_____	_____	
_____	_____	_____	_____	
_____	_____	_____	_____	

21 Ps™

WORLD'S SUREST...FASTEST...SYSTEM FOR MONEY & SUCCESS...MLM CUSTOM GUIDEBOOK

CALENDAR
DAILY & HOURLY ACTIVITIES FOR 6 MONTHS (START AT ANY MONTH)

YEAR: _____ : WEEK 1 of MONTH ____ : 1st Half of Week

PRIORITIES/EVENTS/APPOINTMENTS OF THE WEEK:	Monday Today's Main Focus or Priority	Tuesday Today's Main Focus or Priority	Wednesday Today's Main Focus or Priority
_____ _____ _____ _____ _____	_____ _____ MORNING:	_____ _____ MORNING:	_____ _____ MORNING:
-------------------------------- Small Goal 1: Success(es):	_____ _____ _____ _____ _____	_____ _____ _____ _____ _____	_____ _____ _____ _____ _____
-------------------------------- Small Goal 2: Success(es):	9am 10am 11am 12noon 1pm 2pm	9am 10am 11am 12noon 1pm 2pm	9am 10am 11am 12noon 1pm 2pm
-------------------------------- BIG Goal 1: **Deadline**: _____ Success(es):	3pm 4pm 5pm 6pm 7pm 8pm	3pm 4pm 5pm 6pm 7pm 8pm	3pm 4pm 5pm 6pm 7pm 8pm
Note: Small Goals must support Big Goals which have deadlines. Connect these Big Goals to the Monthly & Yearly Time-lines -------------------------------- WEEKLY TRAINING List at least 1 "P" Focused on:	EVENING/NIGHT: _____ _____ _____ _____	EVENING/NIGHT: _____ _____ _____ _____	EVENING/NIGHT: _____ _____ _____ _____

21 Ps™

WORLD'S SUREST...FASTEST...SYSTEM FOR MONEY & SUCCESS...MLM CUSTOM GUIDEBOOK

CALENDAR
DAILY & HOURLY ACTIVITIES FOR 6 MONTHS (START AT ANY MONTH)

YEAR: _____ : WEEK 1 of MONTH ____ : 2nd Half of Week

Thursday Today's Main Focus or Priority	Friday Today's Main Focus or Priority	Saturday Today's Main Focus or Priority	Sunday Today's Main Focus or Priority	NOTES:
MORNING:	MORNING:	MORNING:	MORNING:	
9am	9am	9am	9am	
10am	10am	10am	10am	
11am	11am	11am	11am	
12noon	12noon	12noon	12noon	
1pm	1pm	1pm	1pm	
2pm	2pm	2pm	2pm	
3pm	3pm	3pm	3pm	
4pm	4pm	4pm	4pm	
5pm	5pm	5pm	5pm	
6pm	6pm	6pm	6pm	
7pm	7pm	7pm	7pm	
8pm	8pm	8pm	8pm	
EVENING/NIGHT:	EVENING/NIGHT:	EVENING/NIGHT:	EVENING/NIGHT:	

21 Ps™

WORLD'S SUREST...FASTEST...SYSTEM FOR MONEY & SUCCESS...MLM CUSTOM GUIDEBOOK

CALENDAR
DAILY & HOURLY ACTIVITIES FOR 6 MONTHS (START AT ANY MONTH)

YEAR: _____ : WEEK 2 of MONTH _____ : 1st Half of Week

PRIORITIES/EVENTS/APPOINTMENTS OF THE WEEK:	Monday Today's Main Focus or Priority	Tuesday Today's Main Focus or Priority	Wednesday Today's Main Focus or Priority
_____	_____	_____	_____
_____	_____	_____	_____
_____	MORNING:	MORNING:	MORNING:
_____	_____	_____	_____
------------------------------------	_____	_____	_____
Small Goal 1:	_____	_____	_____
Success(es):	_____	_____	_____
_____	9am	9am	9am
_____	10am	10am	10am
------------------------------------	11am	11am	11am
Small Goal 2:	12noon	12noon	12noon
Success(es):	1pm	1pm	1pm
_____	2pm	2pm	2pm
_____	3pm	3pm	3pm
------------------------------------	4pm	4pm	4pm
BIG Goal 1:	5pm	5pm	5pm
	6pm	6pm	6pm
Deadline: _____	7pm	7pm	7pm
Success(es):	8pm	8pm	8pm
_____	EVENING/NIGHT:	EVENING/NIGHT:	EVENING/NIGHT:
_____	_____	_____	_____
Note: Small Goals must support Big Goals which have deadlines. Connect these Big Goals to the Monthly & Yearly Time-lines	_____	_____	_____
------------------------------------	_____	_____	_____
WEEKLY TRAINING List at least 1 "P" Focused on:	_____	_____	_____
_____			

21 Ps™

WORLD'S SUREST...FASTEST...SYSTEM FOR MONEY & SUCCESS...MLM CUSTOM GUIDEBOOK

CALENDAR

DAILY & HOURLY ACTIVITIES FOR 6 MONTHS (START AT ANY MONTH)

YEAR: _____ : WEEK 2 of MONTH ____ : 2nd Half of Week

Thursday Today's Main Focus or Priority	Friday Today's Main Focus or Priority	Saturday Today's Main Focus or Priority	Sunday Today's Main Focus or Priority	NOTES:
MORNING:	MORNING:	MORNING:	MORNING:	
9am	9am	9am	9am	
10am	10am	10am	10am	
11am	11am	11am	11am	
12noon	12noon	12noon	12noon	
1pm	1pm	1pm	1pm	
2pm	2pm	2pm	2pm	
3pm	3pm	3pm	3pm	
4pm	4pm	4pm	4pm	
5pm	5pm	5pm	5pm	
6pm	6pm	6pm	6pm	
7pm	7pm	7pm	7pm	
8pm	8pm	8pm	8pm	
EVENING/NIGHT:	EVENING/NIGHT:	EVENING/NIGHT:	EVENING/NIGHT:	

21 Ps™

WORLD'S SUREST...FASTEST...SYSTEM FOR MONEY & SUCCESS...MLM CUSTOM GUIDEBOOK

CALENDAR
DAILY & HOURLY ACTIVITIES FOR 6 MONTHS (START AT ANY MONTH)

YEAR: _____ : WEEK 3 of MONTH _____ : 1st Half of Week

PRIORITIES/EVENTS/APPOINTMENTS OF THE WEEK:	Monday Today's Main Focus or Priority	Tuesday Today's Main Focus or Priority	Wednesday Today's Main Focus or Priority
_____	_____	_____	_____
_____	_____	_____	_____
_____	MORNING:	MORNING:	MORNING:
_____			
_____	_____	_____	_____
------------------------	_____	_____	_____
Small Goal 1:	_____	_____	_____
	_____	_____	_____
Success(es):			
_____	9am	9am	9am
	10am	10am	10am
------------------------	11am	11am	11am
Small Goal 2:	12noon	12noon	12noon
	1pm	1pm	1pm
Success(es):	2pm	2pm	2pm
_____	3pm	3pm	3pm
	4pm	4pm	4pm
------------------------	5pm	5pm	5pm
BIG Goal 1:	6pm	6pm	6pm
Deadline: _____	7pm	7pm	7pm
Success(es):	8pm	8pm	8pm
_____	EVENING/NIGHT:	EVENING/NIGHT:	EVENING/NIGHT:
Note: Small Goals must support Big Goals which have deadlines. Connect these Big Goals to the Monthly & Yearly Time-lines			

WEEKLY TRAINING List at least 1 "P" Focused on:			

21 Ps™

WORLD'S SUREST...FASTEST...SYSTEM FOR MONEY & SUCCESS...MLM CUSTOM GUIDEBOOK

CALENDAR

DAILY & HOURLY ACTIVITIES FOR 6 MONTHS (START AT ANY MONTH)

YEAR: _____ : WEEK 3 of MONTH _____ : 2nd Half of Week

Thursday Today's Main Focus or Priority	Friday Today's Main Focus or Priority	Saturday Today's Main Focus or Priority	Sunday Today's Main Focus or Priority	NOTES:
_____ _____ MORNING: _____ _____ _____ _____	_____ _____ MORNING: _____ _____ _____ _____	_____ _____ MORNING: _____ _____ _____ _____	_____ _____ MORNING: _____ _____ _____ _____	
9am	9am	9am	9am	
10am	10am	10am	10am	
11am	11am	11am	11am	
12noon	12noon	12noon	12noon	
1pm	1pm	1pm	1pm	
2pm	2pm	2pm	2pm	
3pm	3pm	3pm	3pm	
4pm	4pm	4pm	4pm	
5pm	5pm	5pm	5pm	
6pm	6pm	6pm	6pm	
7pm	7pm	7pm	7pm	
8pm	8pm	8pm	8pm	
EVENING/NIGHT: _____ _____ _____ _____ _____	EVENING/NIGHT: _____ _____ _____ _____ _____	EVENING/NIGHT: _____ _____ _____ _____ _____	EVENING/NIGHT: _____ _____ _____ _____ _____	

21 Ps™

WORLD'S SUREST...FASTEST...SYSTEM FOR MONEY & SUCCESS...MLM CUSTOM GUIDEBOOK

CALENDAR
DAILY & HOURLY ACTIVITIES FOR 6 MONTHS (START AT ANY MONTH)

YEAR: _____ : WEEK 4 of MONTH _____ : 1st Half of Week

PRIORITIES/EVENTS/APPOINTMENTS OF THE WEEK:	Monday Today's Main Focus or Priority	Tuesday Today's Main Focus or Priority	Wednesday Today's Main Focus or Priority
_____ _____ _____ _____ _____	_____ _____ MORNING: _____ _____ _____ _____	_____ _____ MORNING: _____ _____ _____ _____	_____ _____ MORNING: _____ _____ _____ _____
-------------------------------------- Small Goal 1: Success(es): _____ _____	9am 10am 11am	9am 10am 11am	9am 10am 11am
-------------------------------------- Small Goal 2: Success(es): _____	12noon 1pm 2pm 3pm	12noon 1pm 2pm 3pm	12noon 1pm 2pm 3pm
-------------------------------------- BIG Goal 1: **Deadline**: _____ Success(es): _____ _____	4pm 5pm 6pm 7pm 8pm EVENING/NIGHT:	4pm 5pm 6pm 7pm 8pm EVENING/NIGHT:	4pm 5pm 6pm 7pm 8pm EVENING/NIGHT:
Note: Small Goals must support Big Goals which have deadlines. Connect these Big Goals to the Monthly & Yearly Time-lines -------------------------------------- WEEKLY TRAINING List at least 1 "P" Focused on: _____	_____ _____ _____ _____	_____ _____ _____ _____	_____ _____ _____ _____

21 Ps™

WORLD'S SUREST...FASTEST...SYSTEM FOR MONEY & SUCCESS...MLM CUSTOM GUIDEBOOK

CALENDAR
DAILY & HOURLY ACTIVITIES FOR 6 MONTHS (START AT ANY MONTH)

YEAR: _____ : WEEK 4 of MONTH _____ : 2nd Half of Week

Thursday Today's Main Focus or Priority	Friday Today's Main Focus or Priority	Saturday Today's Main Focus or Priority	Sunday Today's Main Focus or Priority	NOTES:
MORNING:	MORNING:	MORNING:	MORNING:	
9am	9am	9am	9am	
10am	10am	10am	10am	
11am	11am	11am	11am	
12noon	12noon	12noon	12noon	
1pm	1pm	1pm	1pm	
2pm	2pm	2pm	2pm	
3pm	3pm	3pm	3pm	
4pm	4pm	4pm	4pm	
5pm	5pm	5pm	5pm	
6pm	6pm	6pm	6pm	
7pm	7pm	7pm	7pm	
8pm	8pm	8pm	8pm	
EVENING/NIGHT:	EVENING/NIGHT:	EVENING/NIGHT:	EVENING/NIGHT:	

21 Ps™

WORLD'S SUREST...FASTEST...SYSTEM FOR MONEY & SUCCESS...MLM CUSTOM GUIDEBOOK

CALENDAR
DAILY & HOURLY ACTIVITIES FOR 6 MONTHS (START AT ANY MONTH)

YEAR: _____ : WEEK 5 of MONTH _____ : 1ˢᵗ Half of Week

PRIORITIES/EVENTS/APPOINTMENTS OF THE WEEK:	Monday Today's Main Focus or Priority	Tuesday Today's Main Focus or Priority	Wednesday Today's Main Focus or Priority
_____	_____	_____	_____
_____	_____	_____	_____
_____	MORNING:	MORNING:	MORNING:
_____	_____	_____	_____
-----------------------	_____	_____	_____
Small Goal 1:	_____	_____	_____
Success(es):	_____	_____	_____
_____	9am	9am	9am
_____	10am	10am	10am
-----------------------	11am	11am	11am
Small Goal 2:	12noon	12noon	12noon
Success(es):	1pm	1pm	1pm
_____	2pm	2pm	2pm
_____	3pm	3pm	3pm
_____	4pm	4pm	4pm
-----------------------	5pm	5pm	5pm
BIG Goal 1:	6pm	6pm	6pm
Deadline: _____	7pm	7pm	7pm
Success(es):	8pm	8pm	8pm
_____	EVENING/NIGHT:	EVENING/NIGHT:	EVENING/NIGHT:
Note: Small Goals must support Big Goals which have deadlines. Connect these Big Goals to the Monthly & Yearly Time-lines	_____	_____	_____
-----------------------	_____	_____	_____
WEEKLY TRAINING List at least 1 "P" Focused on:	_____	_____	_____
_____	_____	_____	_____

21 Ps™

WORLD'S SUREST...FASTEST...SYSTEM FOR MONEY & SUCCESS...MLM CUSTOM GUIDEBOOK

CALENDAR
DAILY & HOURLY ACTIVITIES FOR 6 MONTHS (START AT ANY MONTH)

YEAR: _____ : WEEK 5 of MONTH ____ : 2nd Half of Week

Thursday Today's Main Focus or Priority	Friday Today's Main Focus or Priority	Saturday Today's Main Focus or Priority	Sunday Today's Main Focus or Priority	NOTES:
_____	_____	_____	_____	
_____	_____	_____	_____	
MORNING:	MORNING:	MORNING:	MORNING:	
_____	_____	_____	_____	
_____	_____	_____	_____	
_____	_____	_____	_____	
_____	_____	_____	_____	
9am	9am	9am	9am	
10am	10am	10am	10am	
11am	11am	11am	11am	
12noon	12noon	12noon	12noon	
1pm	1pm	1pm	1pm	
2pm	2pm	2pm	2pm	
3pm	3pm	3pm	3pm	
4pm	4pm	4pm	4pm	
5pm	5pm	5pm	5pm	
6pm	6pm	6pm	6pm	
7pm	7pm	7pm	7pm	
8pm	8pm	8pm	8pm	
EVENING/NIGHT:	EVENING/NIGHT:	EVENING/NIGHT:	EVENING/NIGHT:	
_____	_____	_____	_____	
_____	_____	_____	_____	
_____	_____	_____	_____	
_____	_____	_____	_____	
_____	_____	_____	_____	

21 Ps™

WORLD'S SUREST...FASTEST...SYSTEM FOR MONEY & SUCCESS...MLM CUSTOM GUIDEBOOK

CALENDAR
DAILY & HOURLY ACTIVITIES FOR 6 MONTHS (START AT ANY MONTH)

YEAR: _____ : WEEK 1 of MONTH _____ : 1st Half of Week

PRIORITIES/EVENTS/APPOINTMENTS OF THE WEEK:	Monday Today's Main Focus or Priority	Tuesday Today's Main Focus or Priority	Wednesday Today's Main Focus or Priority
_____ _____ _____ _____ ----------------------------------- Small Goal 1: Success(es): _____ _____ ----------------------------------- Small Goal 2: _____ Success(es): _____ _____ ----------------------------------- BIG Goal 1: **Deadline**: _____ Success(es): _____ _____ Note: Small Goals must support Big Goals which have deadlines. Connect these Big Goals to the Monthly & Yearly Time-lines ----------------------------------- WEEKLY TRAINING List at least 1 "P" Focused on: _____	MORNING: ____ ____ ____ ____ 9am 10am 11am 12noon 1pm 2pm 3pm 4pm 5pm 6pm 7pm 8pm EVENING/NIGHT:	MORNING: ____ ____ ____ ____ 9am 10am 11am 12noon 1pm 2pm 3pm 4pm 5pm 6pm 7pm 8pm EVENING/NIGHT:	MORNING: ____ ____ ____ ____ 9am 10am 11am 12noon 1pm 2pm 3pm 4pm 5pm 6pm 7pm 8pm EVENING/NIGHT:

21 Ps™

WORLD'S SUREST...FASTEST...SYSTEM FOR MONEY & SUCCESS...MLM CUSTOM GUIDEBOOK

CALENDAR
DAILY & HOURLY ACTIVITIES FOR 6 MONTHS (START AT ANY MONTH)

YEAR: _____ : WEEK 1 of MONTH ____ : 2nd Half of Week

Thursday Today's Main Focus or Priority	Friday Today's Main Focus or Priority	Saturday Today's Main Focus or Priority	Sunday Today's Main Focus or Priority	NOTES:
MORNING:	MORNING:	MORNING:	MORNING:	
9am	9am	9am	9am	
10am	10am	10am	10am	
11am	11am	11am	11am	
12noon	12noon	12noon	12noon	
1pm	1pm	1pm	1pm	
2pm	2pm	2pm	2pm	
3pm	3pm	3pm	3pm	
4pm	4pm	4pm	4pm	
5pm	5pm	5pm	5pm	
6pm	6pm	6pm	6pm	
7pm	7pm	7pm	7pm	
8pm	8pm	8pm	8pm	
EVENING/NIGHT:	EVENING/NIGHT:	EVENING/NIGHT:	EVENING/NIGHT:	

21 Ps™

WORLD'S SUREST...FASTEST...SYSTEM FOR MONEY & SUCCESS...MLM CUSTOM GUIDEBOOK

CALENDAR
DAILY & HOURLY ACTIVITIES FOR 6 MONTHS (START AT ANY MONTH)

YEAR: _____ : WEEK 2 of MONTH ____ : 1st Half of Week

PRIORITIES/EVENTS/APPOINTMENTS OF THE WEEK:	Monday Today's Main Focus or Priority	Tuesday Today's Main Focus or Priority	Wednesday Today's Main Focus or Priority
_____			
_____			
_____	MORNING:	MORNING:	MORNING:
_____			
- -			
Small Goal 1:			
Success(es):	9am	9am	9am
_____	10am	10am	10am
- -	11am	11am	11am
Small Goal 2:	12noon	12noon	12noon
Success(es):	1pm	1pm	1pm
	2pm	2pm	2pm
_____	3pm	3pm	3pm
- -	4pm	4pm	4pm
BIG Goal 1:	5pm	5pm	5pm
	6pm	6pm	6pm
Deadline: _____	7pm	7pm	7pm
Success(es):	8pm	8pm	8pm
_____	EVENING/NIGHT:	EVENING/NIGHT:	EVENING/NIGHT:
Note: Small Goals must support Big Goals which have deadlines. Connect these Big Goals to the Monthly & Yearly Time-lines			
- -			
WEEKLY TRAINING List at least 1 "P" Focused on:			
_____			

21 Ps™

WORLD'S SUREST...FASTEST...SYSTEM FOR MONEY & SUCCESS...MLM CUSTOM GUIDEBOOK

CALENDAR
DAILY & HOURLY ACTIVITIES FOR 6 MONTHS (START AT ANY MONTH)

YEAR: _____ : WEEK 2 of MONTH _____ : 2nd Half of Week

Thursday Today's Main Focus or Priority	Friday Today's Main Focus or Priority	Saturday Today's Main Focus or Priority	Sunday Today's Main Focus or Priority	NOTES:
_____ _____	_____ _____	_____ _____	_____ _____	
MORNING:	MORNING:	MORNING:	MORNING:	
_____ _____ _____ _____	_____ _____ _____ _____	_____ _____ _____ _____	_____ _____ _____ _____	
9am	9am	9am	9am	
10am	10am	10am	10am	
11am	11am	11am	11am	
12noon	12noon	12noon	12noon	
1pm	1pm	1pm	1pm	
2pm	2pm	2pm	2pm	
3pm	3pm	3pm	3pm	
4pm	4pm	4pm	4pm	
5pm	5pm	5pm	5pm	
6pm	6pm	6pm	6pm	
7pm	7pm	7pm	7pm	
8pm	8pm	8pm	8pm	
EVENING/NIGHT:	EVENING/NIGHT:	EVENING/NIGHT:	EVENING/NIGHT:	
_____ _____ _____ _____ _____	_____ _____ _____ _____ _____	_____ _____ _____ _____ _____	_____ _____ _____ _____ _____	

21 Ps™

WORLD'S SUREST...FASTEST...SYSTEM FOR MONEY & SUCCESS...MLM CUSTOM GUIDEBOOK

CALENDAR
DAILY & HOURLY ACTIVITIES FOR 6 MONTHS (START AT ANY MONTH)

YEAR: _____ : WEEK 3 of MONTH _____ : 1st Half of Week

PRIORITIES/EVENTS/APPOINTMENTS OF THE WEEK:	Monday Today's Main Focus or Priority	Tuesday Today's Main Focus or Priority	Wednesday Today's Main Focus or Priority
_____ _____ _____ _____ _____ -- Small Goal 1: _____ Success(es): _____ _____ -- Small Goal 2: _____ Success(es): _____ _____ -- BIG Goal 1: **Deadline**: _____ Success(es): _____ _____ Note: Small Goals must support Big Goals which have deadlines. Connect these Big Goals to the Monthly & Yearly Time-lines -- WEEKLY TRAINING List at least 1 "P" Focused on: _____	_____ _____ MORNING: _____ _____ _____ _____ 9am _____ 10am _____ 11am _____ 12noon _____ 1pm _____ 2pm _____ 3pm _____ 4pm _____ 5pm _____ 6pm _____ 7pm _____ 8pm _____ EVENING/NIGHT: _____ _____ _____ _____ _____	_____ _____ MORNING: _____ _____ _____ _____ 9am _____ 10am _____ 11am _____ 12noon _____ 1pm _____ 2pm _____ 3pm _____ 4pm _____ 5pm _____ 6pm _____ 7pm _____ 8pm _____ EVENING/NIGHT: _____ _____ _____ _____ _____	_____ _____ MORNING: _____ _____ _____ _____ 9am _____ 10am _____ 11am _____ 12noon _____ 1pm _____ 2pm _____ 3pm _____ 4pm _____ 5pm _____ 6pm _____ 7pm _____ 8pm _____ EVENING/NIGHT: _____ _____ _____ _____ _____

21 Ps™

WORLD'S SUREST...FASTEST...SYSTEM FOR MONEY & SUCCESS...MLM CUSTOM GUIDEBOOK

CALENDAR
DAILY & HOURLY ACTIVITIES FOR 6 MONTHS (START AT ANY MONTH)

YEAR: _____ : WEEK 3 of MONTH _____ : 2nd Half of Week

Thursday Today's Main Focus or Priority	Friday Today's Main Focus or Priority	Saturday Today's Main Focus or Priority	Sunday Today's Main Focus or Priority	NOTES:
_____ _____ MORNING: _____ _____ _____ _____	_____ _____ MORNING: _____ _____ _____ _____	_____ _____ MORNING: _____ _____ _____ _____	_____ _____ MORNING: _____ _____ _____ _____	
9am	9am	9am	9am	
10am	10am	10am	10am	
11am	11am	11am	11am	
12noon	12noon	12noon	12noon	
1pm	1pm	1pm	1pm	
2pm	2pm	2pm	2pm	
3pm	3pm	3pm	3pm	
4pm	4pm	4pm	4pm	
5pm	5pm	5pm	5pm	
6pm	6pm	6pm	6pm	
7pm	7pm	7pm	7pm	
8pm	8pm	8pm	8pm	
EVENING/NIGHT: _____ _____ _____ _____ _____	EVENING/NIGHT: _____ _____ _____ _____ _____	EVENING/NIGHT: _____ _____ _____ _____ _____	EVENING/NIGHT: _____ _____ _____ _____ _____	

21 Ps™

WORLD'S SUREST...FASTEST...SYSTEM FOR MONEY & SUCCESS...MLM CUSTOM GUIDEBOOK

CALENDAR
DAILY & HOURLY ACTIVITIES FOR 6 MONTHS (START AT ANY MONTH)

YEAR: _____ : WEEK 4 of MONTH _____ : 1st Half of Week

PRIORITIES/EVENTS/APPOINTMENTS OF THE WEEK:	Monday Today's Main Focus or Priority	Tuesday Today's Main Focus or Priority	Wednesday Today's Main Focus or Priority
_____	_____	_____	_____
_____	_____	_____	_____
_____	MORNING:	MORNING:	MORNING:
_____	_____	_____	_____
-------------------------------------	_____	_____	_____
Small Goal 1:	_____	_____	_____
Success(es):	_____	_____	_____
_____	9am	9am	9am
_____	10am	10am	10am
-------------------------------------	11am	11am	11am
Small Goal 2:	12noon	12noon	12noon
_____	1pm	1pm	1pm
Success(es):	2pm	2pm	2pm
_____	3pm	3pm	3pm
_____	4pm	4pm	4pm
-------------------------------------	5pm	5pm	5pm
BIG Goal 1:	6pm	6pm	6pm
Deadline: _____	7pm	7pm	7pm
Success(es):	8pm	8pm	8pm
_____	EVENING/NIGHT:	EVENING/NIGHT:	EVENING/NIGHT:
_____	_____	_____	_____
Note: Small Goals must support Big Goals which have deadlines. Connect these Big Goals to the Monthly & Yearly Time-lines	_____	_____	_____
-------------------------------------	_____	_____	_____
WEEKLY TRAINING List at least 1 "P" Focused on:	_____	_____	_____
_____			

21 Ps™

WORLD'S SUREST...FASTEST...SYSTEM FOR MONEY & SUCCESS...MLM CUSTOM GUIDEBOOK

CALENDAR
DAILY & HOURLY ACTIVITIES FOR 6 MONTHS (START AT ANY MONTH)

YEAR: _____ : WEEK 4 of MONTH ____ : 2nd Half of Week

Thursday Today's Main Focus or Priority	Friday Today's Main Focus or Priority	Saturday Today's Main Focus or Priority	Sunday Today's Main Focus or Priority	NOTES:
_____	_____	_____	_____	
_____	_____	_____	_____	
MORNING:	MORNING:	MORNING:	MORNING:	
_____	_____	_____	_____	
_____	_____	_____	_____	
_____	_____	_____	_____	
_____	_____	_____	_____	
9am	9am	9am	9am	
10am	10am	10am	10am	
11am	11am	11am	11am	
12noon	12noon	12noon	12noon	
1pm	1pm	1pm	1pm	
2pm	2pm	2pm	2pm	
3pm	3pm	3pm	3pm	
4pm	4pm	4pm	4pm	
5pm	5pm	5pm	5pm	
6pm	6pm	6pm	6pm	
7pm	7pm	7pm	7pm	
8pm	8pm	8pm	8pm	
EVENING/NIGHT:	EVENING/NIGHT:	EVENING/NIGHT:	EVENING/NIGHT:	
_____	_____	_____	_____	
_____	_____	_____	_____	
_____	_____	_____	_____	
_____	_____	_____	_____	

21 Ps™

WORLD'S SUREST...FASTEST...SYSTEM FOR MONEY & SUCCESS...MLM CUSTOM GUIDEBOOK

CALENDAR
DAILY & HOURLY ACTIVITIES FOR 6 MONTHS (START AT ANY MONTH)

YEAR: _____ : WEEK 5 of MONTH _____ : 1st Half of Week

PRIORITIES/EVENTS/APPOINTMENTS OF THE WEEK:	Monday Today's Main Focus or Priority	Tuesday Today's Main Focus or Priority	Wednesday Today's Main Focus or Priority
_____	_____	_____	_____
_____	_____	_____	_____
_____	MORNING:	MORNING:	MORNING:
_____	_____	_____	_____
---	_____	_____	_____
Small Goal 1:	_____	_____	_____
Success(es):	_____	_____	_____
_____	9am	9am	9am
	10am	10am	10am
_____	11am	11am	11am
---	12noon	12noon	12noon
Small Goal 2:	1pm	1pm	1pm
Success(es):	2pm	2pm	2pm
_____	3pm	3pm	3pm
	4pm	4pm	4pm
_____	5pm	5pm	5pm
---	6pm	6pm	6pm
BIG Goal 1:	7pm	7pm	7pm
Deadline: _____	8pm	8pm	8pm
Success(es):			
_____	EVENING/NIGHT:	EVENING/NIGHT:	EVENING/NIGHT:
_____	_____	_____	_____
Note: Small Goals must support Big Goals which have deadlines. Connect these Big Goals to the Monthly & Yearly Time-lines	_____	_____	_____
---	_____	_____	_____
WEEKLY TRAINING List at least 1 "P" Focused on:	_____	_____	_____
_____			

21 Ps™

WORLD'S SUREST...FASTEST...SYSTEM FOR MONEY & SUCCESS...MLM CUSTOM GUIDEBOOK

CALENDAR
DAILY & HOURLY ACTIVITIES FOR 6 MONTHS (START AT ANY MONTH)

YEAR: _____ : WEEK 5 of MONTH _____ : 2nd Half of Week

Thursday Today's Main Focus or Priority	Friday Today's Main Focus or Priority	Saturday Today's Main Focus or Priority	Sunday Today's Main Focus or Priority	NOTES:
_____ _____ MORNING:	_____ _____ MORNING:	_____ _____ MORNING:	_____ _____ MORNING:	
9am	9am	9am	9am	
10am	10am	10am	10am	
11am	11am	11am	11am	
12noon	12noon	12noon	12noon	
1pm	1pm	1pm	1pm	
2pm	2pm	2pm	2pm	
3pm	3pm	3pm	3pm	
4pm	4pm	4pm	4pm	
5pm	5pm	5pm	5pm	
6pm	6pm	6pm	6pm	
7pm	7pm	7pm	7pm	
8pm	8pm	8pm	8pm	
EVENING/NIGHT:	EVENING/NIGHT:	EVENING/NIGHT:	EVENING/NIGHT:	

21 Ps™

WORLD'S SUREST...FASTEST...SYSTEM FOR MONEY & SUCCESS...MLM CUSTOM GUIDEBOOK

CALENDAR
DAILY & HOURLY ACTIVITIES FOR 6 MONTHS (START AT ANY MONTH)

YEAR: _____ : WEEK 1 of MONTH ____ : 1st Half of Week

PRIORITIES/EVENTS/APPOINTMENTS OF THE WEEK:	Monday Today's Main Focus or Priority	Tuesday Today's Main Focus or Priority	Wednesday Today's Main Focus or Priority
_____			
_____			
_____	MORNING:	MORNING:	MORNING:
_____			

Small Goal 1:			
_____			
Success(es):	9am	9am	9am
_____	10am	10am	10am
------------------------------------	11am	11am	11am
Small Goal 2:	12noon	12noon	12noon
_____	1pm	1pm	1pm
Success(es):	2pm	2pm	2pm
_____	3pm	3pm	3pm
------------------------------------	4pm	4pm	4pm
BIG Goal 1:	5pm	5pm	5pm
	6pm	6pm	6pm
Deadline: _____	7pm	7pm	7pm
Success(es):	8pm	8pm	8pm
_____			
_____	EVENING/NIGHT:	EVENING/NIGHT:	EVENING/NIGHT:
Note: Small Goals must support Big Goals which have deadlines. Connect these Big Goals to the Monthly & Yearly Time-lines			

WEEKLY TRAINING List at least 1 "P" Focused on:			
_____			

21 Ps™

WORLD'S SUREST...FASTEST...SYSTEM FOR MONEY & SUCCESS...MLM CUSTOM GUIDEBOOK

CALENDAR
DAILY & HOURLY ACTIVITIES FOR 6 MONTHS (START AT ANY MONTH)

YEAR: _____ : WEEK 1 of MONTH ____ : 2nd Half of Week

Thursday Today's Main Focus or Priority	Friday Today's Main Focus or Priority	Saturday Today's Main Focus or Priority	Sunday Today's Main Focus or Priority	NOTES:
MORNING:	MORNING:	MORNING:	MORNING:	
9am	9am	9am	9am	
10am	10am	10am	10am	
11am	11am	11am	11am	
12noon	12noon	12noon	12noon	
1pm	1pm	1pm	1pm	
2pm	2pm	2pm	2pm	
3pm	3pm	3pm	3pm	
4pm	4pm	4pm	4pm	
5pm	5pm	5pm	5pm	
6pm	6pm	6pm	6pm	
7pm	7pm	7pm	7pm	
8pm	8pm	8pm	8pm	
EVENING/NIGHT:	EVENING/NIGHT:	EVENING/NIGHT:	EVENING/NIGHT:	

21 Ps™

WORLD'S SUREST...FASTEST...SYSTEM FOR MONEY & SUCCESS...MLM CUSTOM GUIDEBOOK

CALENDAR
DAILY & HOURLY ACTIVITIES FOR 6 MONTHS (START AT ANY MONTH)

YEAR: _____ : WEEK 2 of MONTH ____ : 1st Half of Week

PRIORITIES/EVENTS/APPOINTMENTS OF THE WEEK:	Monday Today's Main Focus or Priority	Tuesday Today's Main Focus or Priority	Wednesday Today's Main Focus or Priority
_____ _____ _____ _____	_____ _____ MORNING: _____ _____ _____ _____	_____ _____ MORNING: _____ _____ _____ _____	_____ _____ MORNING: _____ _____ _____ _____
------------------------------------- Small Goal 1:			
Success(es): _____	9am	9am	9am
_____	10am	10am	10am
-------------------------------------- Small Goal 2:	11am	11am	11am
	12noon	12noon	12noon
_____ Success(es):	1pm	1pm	1pm
_____	2pm	2pm	2pm
_____	3pm	3pm	3pm
-------------------------------------- BIG Goal 1:	4pm	4pm	4pm
	5pm	5pm	5pm
Deadline: _____	6pm	6pm	6pm
Success(es):	7pm	7pm	7pm
_____	8pm	8pm	8pm
_____	EVENING/NIGHT:	EVENING/NIGHT:	EVENING/NIGHT:
Note: Small Goals must support Big Goals which have deadlines. Connect these Big Goals to the Monthly & Yearly Time-lines -------------------------------------- WEEKLY TRAINING List at least 1 "P" Focused on: _____	_____ _____ _____ _____	_____ _____ _____ _____	_____ _____ _____ _____

21 Ps™

WORLD'S SUREST...FASTEST...SYSTEM FOR MONEY & SUCCESS...MLM CUSTOM GUIDEBOOK

CALENDAR
DAILY & HOURLY ACTIVITIES FOR 6 MONTHS (START AT ANY MONTH)

YEAR: _____ : WEEK 2 of MONTH ____ : 2nd Half of Week

Thursday Today's Main Focus or Priority	Friday Today's Main Focus or Priority	Saturday Today's Main Focus or Priority	Sunday Today's Main Focus or Priority	NOTES:
_____	_____	_____	_____	
_____	_____	_____	_____	
MORNING:	MORNING:	MORNING:	MORNING:	
_____	_____	_____	_____	
_____	_____	_____	_____	
_____	_____	_____	_____	
_____	_____	_____	_____	
9am	9am	9am	9am	
10am	10am	10am	10am	
11am	11am	11am	11am	
12noon	12noon	12noon	12noon	
1pm	1pm	1pm	1pm	
2pm	2pm	2pm	2pm	
3pm	3pm	3pm	3pm	
4pm	4pm	4pm	4pm	
5pm	5pm	5pm	5pm	
6pm	6pm	6pm	6pm	
7pm	7pm	7pm	7pm	
8pm	8pm	8pm	8pm	
EVENING/NIGHT:	EVENING/NIGHT:	EVENING/NIGHT:	EVENING/NIGHT:	
_____	_____	_____	_____	
_____	_____	_____	_____	
_____	_____	_____	_____	
_____	_____	_____	_____	
_____	_____	_____	_____	

21 Ps™

WORLD'S SUREST...FASTEST...SYSTEM FOR MONEY & SUCCESS...MLM CUSTOM GUIDEBOOK

CALENDAR
DAILY & HOURLY ACTIVITIES FOR 6 MONTHS (START AT ANY MONTH)

YEAR: _____ : WEEK 3 of MONTH _____ : 1st Half of Week

PRIORITIES/EVENTS/APPOINTMENTS OF THE WEEK:	Monday Today's Main Focus or Priority	Tuesday Today's Main Focus or Priority	Wednesday Today's Main Focus or Priority
_____	_____	_____	_____
_____	_____	_____	_____
_____	MORNING:	MORNING:	MORNING:
_____	_____	_____	_____
--------------------------------	_____	_____	_____
Small Goal 1:	_____	_____	_____
Success(es):	_____	_____	_____
_____	9am	9am	9am
--------------------------------	10am	10am	10am
Small Goal 2:	11am	11am	11am
Success(es):	12noon	12noon	12noon
	1pm	1pm	1pm
_____	2pm	2pm	2pm
_____	3pm	3pm	3pm
--------------------------------	4pm	4pm	4pm
BIG Goal 1:	5pm	5pm	5pm
	6pm	6pm	6pm
Deadline: _____	7pm	7pm	7pm
Success(es):	8pm	8pm	8pm
_____	EVENING/NIGHT:	EVENING/NIGHT:	EVENING/NIGHT:
Note: Small Goals must support Big Goals which have deadlines. Connect these Big Goals to the Monthly & Yearly Time-lines	_____	_____	_____
--------------------------------	_____	_____	_____
WEEKLY TRAINING List at least 1 "P" Focused on:	_____	_____	_____
_____	_____	_____	_____

21 Ps™

WORLD'S SUREST...FASTEST...SYSTEM FOR MONEY & SUCCESS...MLM CUSTOM GUIDEBOOK

CALENDAR
DAILY & HOURLY ACTIVITIES FOR 6 MONTHS (START AT ANY MONTH)

YEAR: _____ : WEEK 3 of MONTH _____ : 2nd Half of Week

Thursday Today's Main Focus or Priority	Friday Today's Main Focus or Priority	Saturday Today's Main Focus or Priority	Sunday Today's Main Focus or Priority	NOTES:
_____	_____	_____	_____	
_____	_____	_____	_____	
MORNING:	MORNING:	MORNING:	MORNING:	
_____	_____	_____	_____	
_____	_____	_____	_____	
_____	_____	_____	_____	
_____	_____	_____	_____	
9am	9am	9am	9am	
10am	10am	10am	10am	
11am	11am	11am	11am	
12noon	12noon	12noon	12noon	
1pm	1pm	1pm	1pm	
2pm	2pm	2pm	2pm	
3pm	3pm	3pm	3pm	
4pm	4pm	4pm	4pm	
5pm	5pm	5pm	5pm	
6pm	6pm	6pm	6pm	
7pm	7pm	7pm	7pm	
8pm	8pm	8pm	8pm	
EVENING/NIGHT:	EVENING/NIGHT:	EVENING/NIGHT:	EVENING/NIGHT:	
_____	_____	_____	_____	
_____	_____	_____	_____	
_____	_____	_____	_____	
_____	_____	_____	_____	
_____	_____	_____	_____	

21 Ps™

WORLD'S SUREST...FASTEST...SYSTEM FOR MONEY & SUCCESS...MLM CUSTOM GUIDEBOOK

CALENDAR
DAILY & HOURLY ACTIVITIES FOR 6 MONTHS (START AT ANY MONTH)

YEAR: _____ : WEEK 4 of MONTH _____ : 1st Half of Week

PRIORITIES/EVENTS/APPOINTMENTS OF THE WEEK:	Monday Today's Main Focus or Priority	Tuesday Today's Main Focus or Priority	Wednesday Today's Main Focus or Priority
_____	_____	_____	_____
_____	_____	_____	_____
_____	MORNING:	MORNING:	MORNING:
_____	_____	_____	_____
---------------------------------	_____	_____	_____
Small Goal 1:	_____	_____	_____
Success(es):	_____	_____	_____
_____	9am	9am	9am
---------------------------------	10am	10am	10am
Small Goal 2:	11am	11am	11am
_____	12noon	12noon	12noon
Success(es):	1pm	1pm	1pm
_____	2pm	2pm	2pm
_____	3pm	3pm	3pm
---------------------------------	4pm	4pm	4pm
BIG Goal 1:	5pm	5pm	5pm
	6pm	6pm	6pm
Deadline: _____	7pm	7pm	7pm
Success(es):	8pm	8pm	8pm
_____	EVENING/NIGHT:	EVENING/NIGHT:	EVENING/NIGHT:
_____	_____	_____	_____
Note: Small Goals must support Big Goals which have deadlines. Connect these Big Goals to the Monthly & Yearly Time-lines	_____	_____	_____
---------------------------------	_____	_____	_____
WEEKLY TRAINING List at least 1 "P" Focused on:	_____	_____	_____
_____	_____	_____	_____

21 Ps™

WORLD'S SUREST...FASTEST...SYSTEM FOR MONEY & SUCCESS...MLM CUSTOM GUIDEBOOK

CALENDAR
DAILY & HOURLY ACTIVITIES FOR 6 MONTHS (START AT ANY MONTH)

YEAR: _____ : WEEK 4 of MONTH _____ : 2nd Half of Week

Thursday Today's Main Focus or Priority	Friday Today's Main Focus or Priority	Saturday Today's Main Focus or Priority	Sunday Today's Main Focus or Priority	NOTES:
_____	_____	_____	_____	
_____	_____	_____	_____	
MORNING:	MORNING:	MORNING:	MORNING:	
_____	_____	_____	_____	
_____	_____	_____	_____	
_____	_____	_____	_____	
_____	_____	_____	_____	
9am	9am	9am	9am	
10am	10am	10am	10am	
11am	11am	11am	11am	
12noon	12noon	12noon	12noon	
1pm	1pm	1pm	1pm	
2pm	2pm	2pm	2pm	
3pm	3pm	3pm	3pm	
4pm	4pm	4pm	4pm	
5pm	5pm	5pm	5pm	
6pm	6pm	6pm	6pm	
7pm	7pm	7pm	7pm	
8pm	8pm	8pm	8pm	
EVENING/NIGHT:	EVENING/NIGHT:	EVENING/NIGHT:	EVENING/NIGHT:	
_____	_____	_____	_____	
_____	_____	_____	_____	
_____	_____	_____	_____	
_____	_____	_____	_____	

21 Ps™

WORLD'S SUREST...FASTEST...SYSTEM FOR MONEY & SUCCESS...MLM CUSTOM GUIDEBOOK

CALENDAR
DAILY & HOURLY ACTIVITIES FOR 6 MONTHS (START AT ANY MONTH)

YEAR: _____ : WEEK 5 of MONTH _____ : 1st Half of Week

PRIORITIES/EVENTS/APPOINTMENTS OF THE WEEK:	Monday Today's Main Focus or Priority	Tuesday Today's Main Focus or Priority	Wednesday Today's Main Focus or Priority
_____	_____	_____	_____
_____	_____	_____	_____
_____			
_____	MORNING:	MORNING:	MORNING:
_____	_____	_____	_____
--	_____	_____	_____
Small Goal 1:	_____	_____	_____
	_____	_____	_____
Success(es):	_____	_____	_____
_____	9am	9am	9am
_____	10am	10am	10am
--	11am	11am	11am
Small Goal 2:	12noon	12noon	12noon
_____	1pm	1pm	1pm
Success(es):	2pm	2pm	2pm
_____	3pm	3pm	3pm
_____	4pm	4pm	4pm
--	5pm	5pm	5pm
BIG Goal 1:	6pm	6pm	6pm
Deadline: _____	7pm	7pm	7pm
Success(es):	8pm	8pm	8pm
_____			
_____	EVENING/NIGHT:	EVENING/NIGHT:	EVENING/NIGHT:
Note: Small Goals must support Big Goals which have deadlines. Connect these Big Goals to the Monthly & Yearly Time-lines	_____	_____	_____
--	_____	_____	_____
WEEKLY TRAINING List at least 1 "P" Focused on:	_____	_____	_____
_____	_____	_____	_____

21 Ps™

WORLD'S SUREST...FASTEST...SYSTEM FOR MONEY & SUCCESS...MLM CUSTOM GUIDEBOOK

CALENDAR
DAILY & HOURLY ACTIVITIES FOR 6 MONTHS (START AT ANY MONTH)

YEAR: _____ : WEEK 5 of MONTH ____ : 2nd Half of Week

Thursday Today's Main Focus or Priority	Friday Today's Main Focus or Priority	Saturday Today's Main Focus or Priority	Sunday Today's Main Focus or Priority	NOTES:
_____	_____	_____	_____	
_____	_____	_____	_____	
MORNING:	MORNING:	MORNING:	MORNING:	
_____	_____	_____	_____	
_____	_____	_____	_____	
_____	_____	_____	_____	
_____	_____	_____	_____	
9am	9am	9am	9am	
10am	10am	10am	10am	
11am	11am	11am	11am	
12noon	12noon	12noon	12noon	
1pm	1pm	1pm	1pm	
2pm	2pm	2pm	2pm	
3pm	3pm	3pm	3pm	
4pm	4pm	4pm	4pm	
5pm	5pm	5pm	5pm	
6pm	6pm	6pm	6pm	
7pm	7pm	7pm	7pm	
8pm	8pm	8pm	8pm	
EVENING/NIGHT:	EVENING/NIGHT:	EVENING/NIGHT:	EVENING/NIGHT:	
_____	_____	_____	_____	
_____	_____	_____	_____	
_____	_____	_____	_____	
_____	_____	_____	_____	

21 Ps™

WORLD'S SUREST...FASTEST...SYSTEM FOR MONEY & SUCCESS...MLM CUSTOM GUIDEBOOK

CALENDAR
DAILY & HOURLY ACTIVITIES FOR 6 MONTHS (START AT ANY MONTH)

YEAR: _____ : WEEK 1 of MONTH _____ : 1st Half of Week

PRIORITIES/EVENTS/APPOINTMENTS OF THE WEEK:	Monday Today's Main Focus or Priority	Tuesday Today's Main Focus or Priority	Wednesday Today's Main Focus or Priority
_____ _____ _____ _____ ------------------------------------ Small Goal 1: Success(es): _____ ------------------------------------ Small Goal 2: Success(es): _____ ------------------------------------ BIG Goal 1: **Deadline**: _____ Success(es): _____ _____ Note: Small Goals must support Big Goals which have deadlines. Connect these Big Goals to the Monthly & Yearly Time-lines ------------------------------------ WEEKLY TRAINING List at least 1 "P" Focused on: _____	_____ _____ MORNING: _____ _____ _____ _____ 9am 10am 11am 12noon 1pm 2pm 3pm 4pm 5pm 6pm 7pm 8pm EVENING/NIGHT: _____ _____ _____ _____	_____ _____ MORNING: _____ _____ _____ _____ 9am 10am 11am 12noon 1pm 2pm 3pm 4pm 5pm 6pm 7pm 8pm EVENING/NIGHT: _____ _____ _____ _____	_____ _____ MORNING: _____ _____ _____ _____ 9am 10am 11am 12noon 1pm 2pm 3pm 4pm 5pm 6pm 7pm 8pm EVENING/NIGHT: _____ _____ _____ _____

21 Ps™

WORLD'S SUREST...FASTEST...SYSTEM FOR MONEY & SUCCESS...MLM CUSTOM GUIDEBOOK

CALENDAR
DAILY & HOURLY ACTIVITIES FOR 6 MONTHS (START AT ANY MONTH)

YEAR: _____ : WEEK 1 of MONTH ____ : 2nd Half of Week

Thursday Today's Main Focus or Priority	Friday Today's Main Focus or Priority	Saturday Today's Main Focus or Priority	Sunday Today's Main Focus or Priority	NOTES:
MORNING:	MORNING:	MORNING:	MORNING:	
9am	9am	9am	9am	
10am	10am	10am	10am	
11am	11am	11am	11am	
12noon	12noon	12noon	12noon	
1pm	1pm	1pm	1pm	
2pm	2pm	2pm	2pm	
3pm	3pm	3pm	3pm	
4pm	4pm	4pm	4pm	
5pm	5pm	5pm	5pm	
6pm	6pm	6pm	6pm	
7pm	7pm	7pm	7pm	
8pm	8pm	8pm	8pm	
EVENING/NIGHT:	EVENING/NIGHT:	EVENING/NIGHT:	EVENING/NIGHT:	

21 Ps™

WORLD'S SUREST...FASTEST...SYSTEM FOR MONEY & SUCCESS...MLM CUSTOM GUIDEBOOK

CALENDAR
DAILY & HOURLY ACTIVITIES FOR 6 MONTHS (START AT ANY MONTH)

YEAR: _____ : WEEK 2 of MONTH _____ : 1st Half of Week

PRIORITIES/EVENTS/APPOINTMENTS OF THE WEEK:	Monday Today's Main Focus or Priority	Tuesday Today's Main Focus or Priority	Wednesday Today's Main Focus or Priority
_____	_____	_____	_____
_____	_____	_____	_____
_____	MORNING:	MORNING:	MORNING:
_____	_____	_____	_____
-------------------------------------	_____	_____	_____
Small Goal 1:	_____	_____	_____
_____	_____	_____	_____
Success(es):	9am	9am	9am
_____	10am	10am	10am
_____	11am	11am	11am
-------------------------------------	12noon	12noon	12noon
Small Goal 2:	1pm	1pm	1pm
_____	2pm	2pm	2pm
Success(es):	3pm	3pm	3pm
_____	4pm	4pm	4pm
_____	5pm	5pm	5pm
-------------------------------------	6pm	6pm	6pm
BIG Goal 1:	7pm	7pm	7pm
Deadline: _____	8pm	8pm	8pm
Success(es):			
_____	EVENING/NIGHT:	EVENING/NIGHT:	EVENING/NIGHT:
_____	_____	_____	_____
Note: Small Goals must support Big Goals which have deadlines. Connect these Big Goals to the Monthly & Yearly Time-lines	_____	_____	_____
-------------------------------------	_____	_____	_____
WEEKLY TRAINING List at least 1 "P" Focused on:	_____	_____	_____
_____	_____	_____	_____

21 Ps™

WORLD'S SUREST...FASTEST...SYSTEM FOR MONEY & SUCCESS...MLM CUSTOM GUIDEBOOK

CALENDAR
DAILY & HOURLY ACTIVITIES FOR 6 MONTHS (START AT ANY MONTH)

YEAR: _____ : WEEK 2 of MONTH ____ : 2nd Half of Week

Thursday Today's Main Focus or Priority	Friday Today's Main Focus or Priority	Saturday Today's Main Focus or Priority	Sunday Today's Main Focus or Priority	NOTES:
_____	_____	_____	_____	
_____	_____	_____	_____	
MORNING:	MORNING:	MORNING:	MORNING:	
_____	_____	_____	_____	
_____	_____	_____	_____	
_____	_____	_____	_____	
_____	_____	_____	_____	
9am	9am	9am	9am	
10am	10am	10am	10am	
11am	11am	11am	11am	
12noon	12noon	12noon	12noon	
1pm	1pm	1pm	1pm	
2pm	2pm	2pm	2pm	
3pm	3pm	3pm	3pm	
4pm	4pm	4pm	4pm	
5pm	5pm	5pm	5pm	
6pm	6pm	6pm	6pm	
7pm	7pm	7pm	7pm	
8pm	8pm	8pm	8pm	
EVENING/NIGHT:	EVENING/NIGHT:	EVENING/NIGHT:	EVENING/NIGHT:	
_____	_____	_____	_____	
_____	_____	_____	_____	
_____	_____	_____	_____	
_____	_____	_____	_____	

21 Ps™

WORLD'S SUREST...FASTEST...SYSTEM FOR MONEY & SUCCESS...MLM CUSTOM GUIDEBOOK

CALENDAR
DAILY & HOURLY ACTIVITIES FOR 6 MONTHS (START AT ANY MONTH)

YEAR: _____ : WEEK 3 of MONTH ____ : 1ˢᵗ Half of Week

PRIORITIES/EVENTS/APPOINTMENTS OF THE WEEK:	Monday Today's Main Focus or Priority	Tuesday Today's Main Focus or Priority	Wednesday Today's Main Focus or Priority
_____	_____	_____	_____
_____	_____	_____	_____
_____	MORNING:	MORNING:	MORNING:
_____	_____	_____	_____
------------------------------	_____	_____	_____
Small Goal 1:	_____	_____	_____
Success(es):	_____	_____	_____
_____	9am	9am	9am
_____	10am	10am	10am
------------------------------	11am	11am	11am
Small Goal 2:	12noon	12noon	12noon
Success(es):	1pm	1pm	1pm
_____	2pm	2pm	2pm
_____	3pm	3pm	3pm
------------------------------	4pm	4pm	4pm
BIG Goal 1:	5pm	5pm	5pm
Deadline: _____	6pm	6pm	6pm
Success(es):	7pm	7pm	7pm
_____	8pm	8pm	8pm
_____	EVENING/NIGHT:	EVENING/NIGHT:	EVENING/NIGHT:
Note: Small Goals must support Big Goals which have deadlines. Connect these Big Goals to the Monthly & Yearly Time-lines	_____	_____	_____
------------------------------	_____	_____	_____
WEEKLY TRAINING List at least 1 "P" Focused on:	_____	_____	_____
_____	_____	_____	_____

21 Ps™

WORLD'S SUREST...FASTEST...SYSTEM FOR MONEY & SUCCESS...MLM CUSTOM GUIDEBOOK

CALENDAR
DAILY & HOURLY ACTIVITIES FOR 6 MONTHS (START AT ANY MONTH)

YEAR: _____ : WEEK 3 of MONTH _____ : 2nd Half of Week

Thursday Today's Main Focus or Priority	Friday Today's Main Focus or Priority	Saturday Today's Main Focus or Priority	Sunday Today's Main Focus or Priority	NOTES:
_____ _____	_____ _____	_____ _____	_____ _____	
MORNING:	MORNING:	MORNING:	MORNING:	
9am	9am	9am	9am	
10am	10am	10am	10am	
11am	11am	11am	11am	
12noon	12noon	12noon	12noon	
1pm	1pm	1pm	1pm	
2pm	2pm	2pm	2pm	
3pm	3pm	3pm	3pm	
4pm	4pm	4pm	4pm	
5pm	5pm	5pm	5pm	
6pm	6pm	6pm	6pm	
7pm	7pm	7pm	7pm	
8pm	8pm	8pm	8pm	
EVENING/NIGHT:	EVENING/NIGHT:	EVENING/NIGHT:	EVENING/NIGHT:	

21 Ps™

WORLD'S SUREST...FASTEST...SYSTEM FOR MONEY & SUCCESS...MLM CUSTOM GUIDEBOOK

CALENDAR
DAILY & HOURLY ACTIVITIES FOR 6 MONTHS (START AT ANY MONTH)

YEAR: _____ : WEEK 4 of MONTH _____ : 1st Half of Week

PRIORITIES/EVENTS/APPOINTMENTS OF THE WEEK:	Monday Today's Main Focus or Priority	Tuesday Today's Main Focus or Priority	Wednesday Today's Main Focus or Priority
_____	_____	_____	_____
_____	_____	_____	_____
_____	MORNING:	MORNING:	MORNING:
_____	_____	_____	_____
--------------------------------	_____	_____	_____
Small Goal 1:	_____	_____	_____
_____	_____	_____	_____
Success(es):	9am	9am	9am
_____	10am	10am	10am
_____	11am	11am	11am
--------------------------------	12noon	12noon	12noon
Small Goal 2:	1pm	1pm	1pm
_____	2pm	2pm	2pm
Success(es):	3pm	3pm	3pm
_____	4pm	4pm	4pm
--------------------------------	5pm	5pm	5pm
BIG Goal 1:	6pm	6pm	6pm
Deadline: _____	7pm	7pm	7pm
Success(es):	8pm	8pm	8pm
_____	EVENING/NIGHT:	EVENING/NIGHT:	EVENING/NIGHT:

Note: Small Goals must support Big Goals which have deadlines. Connect these Big Goals to the Monthly & Yearly Time-lines
----
WEEKLY TRAINING
List at least 1 "P" Focused on:

21 Ps™

WORLD'S SUREST...FASTEST...SYSTEM FOR MONEY & SUCCESS...MLM CUSTOM GUIDEBOOK

CALENDAR
DAILY & HOURLY ACTIVITIES FOR 6 MONTHS (START AT ANY MONTH)

YEAR: _____ : WEEK 4 of MONTH ____ : 2nd Half of Week

Thursday Today's Main Focus or Priority	Friday Today's Main Focus or Priority	Saturday Today's Main Focus or Priority	Sunday Today's Main Focus or Priority	NOTES:
MORNING:	MORNING:	MORNING:	MORNING:	
9am	9am	9am	9am	
10am	10am	10am	10am	
11am	11am	11am	11am	
12noon	12noon	12noon	12noon	
1pm	1pm	1pm	1pm	
2pm	2pm	2pm	2pm	
3pm	3pm	3pm	3pm	
4pm	4pm	4pm	4pm	
5pm	5pm	5pm	5pm	
6pm	6pm	6pm	6pm	
7pm	7pm	7pm	7pm	
8pm	8pm	8pm	8pm	
EVENING/NIGHT:	EVENING/NIGHT:	EVENING/NIGHT:	EVENING/NIGHT:	

21 Ps™

WORLD'S SUREST...FASTEST...SYSTEM FOR MONEY & SUCCESS...MLM CUSTOM GUIDEBOOK

CALENDAR
DAILY & HOURLY ACTIVITIES FOR 6 MONTHS (START AT ANY MONTH)

YEAR: _____ : WEEK 5 of MONTH _____ : 1st Half of Week

PRIORITIES/EVENTS/APPOINTMENTS OF THE WEEK:	Monday Today's Main Focus or Priority	Tuesday Today's Main Focus or Priority	Wednesday Today's Main Focus or Priority
_____	_____	_____	_____
_____	_____	_____	_____
_____			
_____	MORNING:	MORNING:	MORNING:
---	_____	_____	_____
Small Goal 1:	_____	_____	_____
	_____	_____	_____
Success(es):	_____	_____	_____
_____	9am	9am	9am
_____	10am	10am	10am
---	11am	11am	11am
Small Goal 2:	12noon	12noon	12noon
_____	1pm	1pm	1pm
Success(es):	2pm	2pm	2pm
_____	3pm	3pm	3pm
_____	4pm	4pm	4pm
---	5pm	5pm	5pm
BIG Goal 1:	6pm	6pm	6pm
Deadline: _____	7pm	7pm	7pm
Success(es):	8pm	8pm	8pm
_____			
_____	EVENING/NIGHT:	EVENING/NIGHT:	EVENING/NIGHT:
Note: Small Goals must support Big Goals which have deadlines. Connect these Big Goals to the Monthly & Yearly Time-lines	_____	_____	_____
---	_____	_____	_____
WEEKLY TRAINING List at least 1 "P" Focused on:	_____	_____	_____
_____	_____	_____	_____

21 Ps™

WORLD'S SUREST...FASTEST...SYSTEM FOR MONEY & SUCCESS...MLM CUSTOM GUIDEBOOK

CALENDAR
DAILY & HOURLY ACTIVITIES FOR 6 MONTHS (START AT ANY MONTH)

YEAR: _____ : WEEK 5 of MONTH ____ : 2nd Half of Week

Thursday Today's Main Focus or Priority	Friday Today's Main Focus or Priority	Saturday Today's Main Focus or Priority	Sunday Today's Main Focus or Priority	NOTES:
MORNING:	MORNING:	MORNING:	MORNING:	
9am	9am	9am	9am	
10am	10am	10am	10am	
11am	11am	11am	11am	
12noon	12noon	12noon	12noon	
1pm	1pm	1pm	1pm	
2pm	2pm	2pm	2pm	
3pm	3pm	3pm	3pm	
4pm	4pm	4pm	4pm	
5pm	5pm	5pm	5pm	
6pm	6pm	6pm	6pm	
7pm	7pm	7pm	7pm	
8pm	8pm	8pm	8pm	
EVENING/NIGHT:	EVENING/NIGHT:	EVENING/NIGHT:	EVENING/NIGHT:	

21 Ps™

WORLD'S SUREST...FASTEST...SYSTEM FOR MONEY & SUCCESS...MLM CUSTOM GUIDEBOOK

21 Ps™

WORLD'S SUREST...FASTEST...SYSTEM FOR MONEY & SUCCESS...MLM CUSTOM GUIDEBOOK

RESOURCES

21 TRAINERS AND LEGENDS

AMONG

(MLM) SUCCESS PRACTITIONERS

21 Ps™

WORLD'S SUREST...FASTEST...SYSTEM FOR MONEY & SUCCESS...MLM CUSTOM GUIDEBOOK

RESOURCES
21 TRAINERS AND LEGENDS
(Listed Alphabetically by Last Name)

GREG ARNOLD (Article as contributed in Dr. Joe Rubino's *The Ultimate Guide to Network Marketing: 37 Top Network Marketing Income-Earners Share Their Most Preciously-Guarded Secrets to Building Extreme Wealth,* 2005, Wiley), "Leadership in an All-Volunteer Army". Arnold was in the military when he discovered MLM, eventually building an organization of over 1,000 Representatives in less than a year. Arnold has become a best-selling Author and a popular Trainer and Consultant.

MARY CHRISTENSEN (2007), *Be a Network Marketing Superstar: The One Book You Need to Make More Money Than You Ever Thought Possible,* (with Wayne Christensen) AMACOM Publishers. Mary Christensen has over 25 years of successful experience in MLM, recruiting more than 1,000 people in her first year from zero. Her books and trainings are practical and powerful.

JIM COLLINS (2011 Kindle Edition), *Good to Great: Why Some Companies Make The Leap...And Others Don't*, CL Business. Collins authored and led the definitive management study, conducted by a diverse team of researchers for over 5 years. Collins describes and offers prescriptions for company greatness that stands the test of time and circumstance.

COMM, JOEL (2010), *Twitter Power 2.0: How to Dominate Your Market One Tweet at a Time*, Wiley. The social media phenomenon is analyzed in detail with powerful implications for MLM in the areas of building trust, value and community, and potentially countless "Followers" of a product or service and business opportunities.

STEVEN R. COVEY (1989), *The 7 Habits of Highly Effective People: Powerful Lessons in Personal Change*, Simon & Schuster, Inc. The "7 Habits" is now a timeless classic of universal principles of behavior and practices of private and public success that has sold over 10 million copies.

MARK EARLS (2009), *Herd: How to Change Mass Behavior by Harnessing Our True Nature*, Wiley. A cutting edge work on marketing, advertising and word-of-mouth programs with some surprising, counter-intuitive and multi-cultural findings.

RANDY GAGE (2009), *How to Build a Multi-Level Money Machine – 4th Edition*, Prime Concepts Group, Inc. Gage an admitted high-school dropout is one of the truly accomplished MLM Practitioners and highly sought-after Trainers. His systems have proven long-lasting success earning Gage tens of millions of dollars in 20 years.

MICHAEL A. JANKE (2000), *Power Living: Mastering the Art of Self-Discipline*, Special Operations Publishing. Janke was a Navy SEAL Commando who became a professional speaker, trainer and consultant to Fortune 500 Companies.

JOHN KALENCH (1990), *Being the Best You Can Be in MLM: How to Train Your Way to the Top in Multi-Level/Network Marketing – America's Fastest-Growing Industry*, MIM Publications. Kalench became a leading trainer in MLM after building 3 highly profitable distributorships in 8 years.

21 Ps™

WORLD'S SUREST...FASTEST...SYSTEM FOR MONEY & SUCCESS...MLM CUSTOM GUIDEBOOK

RESOURCES
21 TRAINERS AND LEGENDS
-Continued-

JAY CONRAD LEVINSON (2008), *Guerilla Multilevel Marketing: 100 Low-Cost Tactics for Growing Your Network and Advancing to the Top of Your Pay Plan* (with James Dillehay and Marcella Vonn Harting), Warm Snow Publishing. Levinson has written over 25 books including *Guerilla Marketing* Books which have sold over 15 Million Copies.

BRUCE LIPTON, PhD (2005), *The Biology of Belief: Unleashing the Power of Consciousness, Matter & Miracles*, Mountain of Love/Elite Books. Dr. Lipton is a leading figure in the science of Epigenetics.

DAVID NIVEN, PhD (2002), *The 100 Simple Secrets of Successful People: What Scientists Have Learned and How You Can Use It*, Harper Collins. The "secrets" of this book are backed by studies and scientific research.

MICHAEL OLIVER (2010) *How to Sell Network Marketing Without Fear, Anxiety or Losing Your Friends!* www.naturalselling.com Publishers. Oliver is an advocate of "natural selling" that makes consultative selling empowering and highly effective for MLM Representatives and Consumers alike.

ANTHONY ROBBINS (2008 Kindle Edition), *Unlimited Power: The New Science of Personal Achievement*, Free Press. A classic book on motivation and success from a legendary motivational performer to hundreds of thousands and author of books to several millions.

DR. JOE RUBINO (2003), *15 Secrets Every Network Marketer Must Know: Essential Elements and Skills Required to Achieve 6- and 7-Figure Success in Network Marketing* (with John Terhune). Rubino is a dentist-turned-MLM Practitioner who became extraordinarily successful in business, training and writing books.

JAN RUHE (Article as contributed in Dr. Joe Rubino's *The Ultimate Guide to Network Marketing: 37 Top Network Marketing Income-Earners Share Their Most Preciously-Guarded Secrets to Building Extreme Wealth*, 2005, Wiley), "Party Your Way to the Top of Network Marketing". Ruhe is a very much active veteran of Network Marketing who has been extremely successful with Discovery Toys MLM for over 30 years! Jan Ruhe is still often the top paid Distributor in her Company.

ALVIN TOFFLER (2006), *Revolutionary Wealth: How It will Be Created and How It Will Change Our Lives* (with Heidi Toffler), Doubleday. Toffler is a thinker, futurist and author who contributed to the global English lexicon the terms "Future Shock", "Third Wave" and "Prosumer" from his international best-selling works.

ECKHART TOLLE (2009 Kindle Edition), *The Power of Now*, New World Library. Eckhart writes, lectures and practices the principles of the essence of Being which is the eternal and simple present. In the processes of MLM existence and success, the power of now can change lives and create results for the best.

DR. DON VOLMER (Article as contributed in Dr. Joe Rubino's *The Ultimate Guide to Network Marketing: 37 Top Network Marketing Income-Earners Share Their Most Preciously-Guarded Secrets to Building Extreme Wealth*, 2005, Wiley), "Building Your Network Marketing with Trade Shows, Booths and Fairs" (with Mary Lou Vollmer). Volmer is a dentist who has found his niche in special MLM products that create great incomes!

ZIG ZIGLAR (2006), *Network Marketing For Dummies* (with John P. Hayes, PhD), Wiley. Ziglar is the legendary motivational speaker and author of *See You at the Top* which has sold over 1.7 million copies.

21 Ps™

WORLD'S SUREST...FASTEST...SYSTEM FOR MONEY & SUCCESS...MLM CUSTOM GUIDEBOOK

21 Ps™

WORLD'S SUREST...FASTEST...SYSTEM FOR MONEY & SUCCESS...MLM CUSTOM GUIDEBOOK

About the Author

Nelson Abaya received his Bachelor of Arts Degree in Literature and Psychology from the University of California, Berkeley, and a Master of Science Degree in International Business from Saint Mary's College of California. He is a legacy LEED AP (Leadership in Energy and Environmental Design Accredited Professional), United States Green Building Council, Washington D.C.

This title (21 Ps Book) and two topical books by the author are also **available** on **amazon.com**, **createspace.com** and **wowresumes.net**: *The 5 Factors of Green Wealth* (2009) and *WOW! Resumes: Get Great Jobs, Extra Income and Happiness!* (2011-2012 Edition). Nelson Abaya is a personal coach and trainer available to success-seeking individuals and organizations.

The Triple Guarantees

In addition to the Money-Back Guarantee available to individual Book Purchasers, there are second and third guarantees for organizations that use this Book for group trainings.

Teams with 10 to 99 MLM Representatives who use the Author or Associates as their Trainers in the System of "21 Ps" are guaranteed contractually to double the Group's Income *and* double the Group's total Recruits in 60 days or Trainer fees and Books are free! The Training includes 2 "SUDU" (Super Duplication) 30-Day Drives.

Teams with 100 or more MLM Representatives who use the Author or Associates as their Trainers are guaranteed contractually to triple the Group's Gross Income in 100 days or Trainer fees and Books are free! The Training includes 3 "SUDU" (Super Duplication) 30-Day Drives.

There will be a Contract to stipulate exact fees, exact charges and exact results. Please contact the Author at 888-503-3133 or email: nelsonabaya@21PsMLM.Com for more details and availability.

21 Ps™

WORLD'S SUREST...FASTEST...SYSTEM FOR MONEY & SUCCESS...MLM CUSTOM GUIDEBOOK

FINAL / MISCELLANEOUS NOTES

21 Ps™

WORLD'S SUREST...FASTEST...SYSTEM FOR MONEY & SUCCESS...MLM CUSTOM GUIDEBOOK

FINAL / MISCELLANEOUS NOTES

21 Ps™
WORLD'S SUREST...FASTEST...SYSTEM FOR MONEY & SUCCESS...MLM CUSTOM GUIDEBOOK

FINAL / MISCELLANEOUS NOTES